ABOUT THIS BOOK

Living Library has been compiled to celebrate the official opening in March 2005 of the new building of the Utrecht University Library (UBU) in the Netherlands. The building was designed by Wiel Arets Architect & Associates.

The book focuses not only on the new building itself and the way its visitors have brought it to life, but also on its inner world: the history of the UBU and its collection, its current and future use, as well as the broader cultural context of libraries internationally. It is precisely this unusual combination that makes Living Library an exceptional book.

Interviews, photographs, architectural drawings, essays and short texts, film stills, artworks, statistics, maps and cartoons illustrate and address these topics in various ways and from different points of view. The result is a compilation of fragments, very diverse and often surprising. Book designer Irma Boom accepted the challenge of shaping these various parts into a single entity. She has made the interweaving of the book's two main components both visible and tangible. The most extensive part, dealing with the new library, is printed on slightly larger, thicker pages. A first quick flick through the book reveals the new building itself, but by turning the pages one by one, the 'inside' story of this library, and libraries in general, unfolds on the interleaving pages.

The main section of the book takes the reader on a tour through the building floor by floor. Having taken in the façade and entered the building, we find ourselves in the entrance hall. From there we take the staircase and explore each level, winding our way right to the top. Each floor is represented by a wealth of source material, including a dialogue between architect Wiel Arets and client Bas Savenije, a proposal by visual artist Pierre Huyghe for an installation in the library's central hall, and a text by Adriaan Geuze of West 8 on the design of the library's courtyard. Also included are essays about the building by architecture critics Roemer van Toorn and Marc Dubois. An article by Bas Savenije presents a vision of the future of university libraries.

The slightly smaller and thinner interior pages dispersed throughout the book deal with the world of the UBU: its collection and history, different modes of access to information, and comments on the future of the library in a digitised world. Other topics here relate to the cultural associations that consciously and unconsciously spring to mind whenever we think of libraries.

The cultural significance of libraries and the 'love' they inspire are highlighted in György Konrád's essay In the Library, written especially for this book and read by him at the official opening of the library, and a photo essay of international, historic libraries by renowned photographer Candida Höfer.

Wiel Arets interviews architects of other libraries. With international colleagues Toyo Ito, Jacques Herzog, Dominique Perrault and Rem Koolhaas he discusses the aspects that affected the way they created their libraries.

This 'inner' section also presents artworks centred on the transfer of information through words, letters or numbers, in a non-traditional way.

Living Library aims to show how much the library, both the new Utrecht University Library as well as other libraries, appeal to our imagination, not only as an institution but also as a phenomenon in society, and will continue to do so.

The Editor

Tubm

I found I had

thoug

there

was nobody

use my

a strange land; and

father, my mo

The Illuminated Manuscript

David Small's Illuminated Manuscript explores the communicative possibilities of spatialized language in the electronic media. Sonar sensors allow visitors to run their hands over a handbound book and to disrupt, combine and manipulate the text on each page, inscribing themselves into the virtual space of the book.

www.davidsmall.com/projects
(last accessed 10 March 2005)

Library Bill of Rights

The American Library Association affirms that all libraries are forums for information and ideas, and that the following basic policies should guide their services.

I
Books and other library resources should be provided for the interest, information, and enlightenment of all people of the community the library serves. Materials should not be excluded because of the origin, background, or views of those contributing to their creation.

II
Libraries should provide materials and information presenting all points of view on current and historical issues. Materials should not be proscribed or removed because of partisan or doctrinal disapproval.

III
Libraries should challenge censorship in the fulfillment of their responsibility to provide information and enlightenment.

IV
Libraries should cooperate with all persons and groups concerned with resisting abridgment of free expression and free access to ideas.

V
A person's right to use a library should not be denied or abridged because of origin, age, background, or views.

VI
Libraries which make exhibit spaces and meeting rooms available to the public they serve should make such facilities available on an equitable basis, regardless of the beliefs or affiliations of individuals or groups requesting their use.

American Library Association
www.ala.org/ala/oif/statementspols/statementsif/librarybillrights.htm>
(last accessed 10 March 2005)

Previous page:
David Small, The Illuminated Manuscript, 2002
Commissioned work for Documenta 11 in Kassel, Germany

CONTENTS

The Story of the Butterfly Book 1

ABOUT THIS BOOK 10

BEING THERE 20
Preface
Bas Savenije

Utrecht Psalter 21
On the Janskerk and Palace of Lodewijk Napoleon 31
The Zwolle Bible 41
The Internet Archive, Brewster Kahle, a man with a mission,
discusses the digital library of the future 61

IN THE LIBRARY 74
György Konrád

Catalogues 91

BUILDING A LIVING LIBRARY 134
Dialogue Wiel Arets and Bas Savenije

The Founding of the Utrecht University Library 152
Wiel Arets interviews Toyo Ito Sendai, Mediatheque 161
Wiel Arets interviews Dominique Perrault, Bibliothèque National de France 171
Wiel Arets interviews Jacques Herzog, Eberswalde Technical School Library 181
Wiel Arets interviews Rem Koolhaas, Seattle Public Library 191

CLOUDS 194
Wiel Arets

FLYING STONES 198
Project for the Library
Pierre Huyghe

THE QUASI-OBJECT 204
Purity and Provocation in Wiel Arets's
Utrecht University Library
Roemer van Toorn

International Libraries Candida Höfer 211, 221, 222, 231, 232, 241, 242
The Library through History 212
Paul Otlet, Forefather of Information Architecture 251

**PERSPECTIVES WITH A
PIRANESIAN DIMENSION** 261
Marc Dubois

THE LIVING ROOM OF THE UNIVERSITY 310
Dialogue Aryan Sikkema and Art Zaaijer

WILLOWS ON CONCRETE AND GLASS 358

Mulberry Trees growing from Hell 377
West 8

MORE THAN A GATEWAY 381
The Role of Future University Libraries
Bas Savenije

The Resistance Movement at the UBU 409

ARCHITECT 449
& Advisors & Contractors
Facts & Figures

Bibliography 451

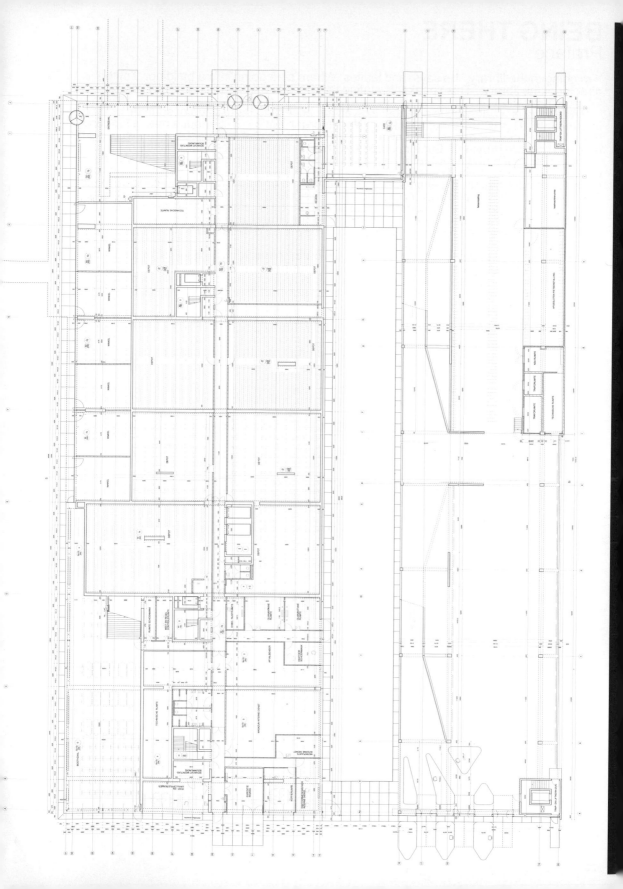

BEING THERE
Preface

"I'm going to the library," he says, and leaves. Where's he going? To a building. "I'm the director of the library." This speaker is stating that he is someone in charge. Of what? Of an organisation.

"The library is a gateway to science. It gives me access to thousands of sources of information." This is not about a building. Nor an organisation. It is about a role, a function. For a library's customers, the organisation is of little interest: it is a mechanism that ensures that services are provided. But for customers, the function is essential. So is the building.

The function of a university library is to provide scientific information. Increasingly, this data is available digitally. These days, you don't even need to visit the library building to consult this information. It can be accessed both from a university workplace and from home. The library (as organisation) is concerned with the accessibility of information. But it does more: selection, classification, quality assessment, storage, assistance in searching, and alerting. The ideal is to organise these services so that they dovetail seamlessly with customers' activities (education and research). They should seem perfectly natural; present yet invisible.

The human face of the library lies in its role as partner in science: cooperation and interaction that are as close as possible to education and research.

As a building, the library prefers not to be invisible. In fact it needs to be a distinct presence on the campus. A symbol for the function of the library in all its aspects. Of which the new is an outstanding example.

The physical aspects of the provision of information are clearly visible. The depots with their many kilometres of information are not hidden away underground but hovezws the eye to the information. The library staff are also a distinct presence. They don't work in an office block, but in a real library. This is true both of the counter staff and those who work, metaphorically, behind the scenes.

The auditorium will become a cultural centre for De Uithof university campus. The library as a whole is a place of study and also a place to meet. This is not a paradox but a lively synthesis. What was a challenge at the design stage, has now become an essential element of the magnetism of the UBU.

The UBU is a living library. And as a living library it has many faces. Some of these faces can only be understood from a historical background. Some can only be appreciated within their environment. Others are somewhat futuristic. We proudly present them all to you.

Bas Savenije
Director of the Library

ETCIBAUITILLOSEXADIPEFRU MENI · ETDEPETRAMELLE SATURAUITEOS ·

LXXXI PSALMUS ASAPH

DSSTETITINSINA
GOGADEORUM · INMIDI
OAUTEMDEOSDIIUDICAT;
UISQUEQUOIUDICATISINIQUI
TATEM · ETFACIESPECCATORU
SUMITIS DIAPSALMA
IUDICATEEGENOETPUPILLO
HUMILEMETPAUPEREMINIS
TIFICATE

ERIPITEPAUPEREMETEGENU
DEMANUPECCATORISLIBERATE
NESCIERUNTNEQUEINTELLEX
ERUNT · INTENEBRISAM
BULANT · MOUEBUNTUROM
NIAFUNDAMENTATERRAE
EGODIXIDIIESTIS · ETFILII
EXCELSIOMNES;
UOSAUTEMSICUTHOMINES

Utrecht Psalter

The Utrecht Psalter is the showpiece of Utrecht University Library (UBU). It is one of the masterpieces of Western medieval art and almost certainly the most important book kept in the Netherlands. The book's fame is due to its 166 pen drawings which are executed with remarkable dynamism and vibrant energy. It was probably made in the Benedictine Abbey of Hautvillers near Reims, France, around 820-835. The book is what is known as a Psalter or Psalterium, a manuscript containing the text of the Book of Psalms. In this example the psalm texts are visualised very literally. Text and images are interwoven in a way which reminds one of present-day cartoon stories. After some considerable travels the book was left to the Utrecht University Library in the early 18th century. The name of the manuscript derives from its present depository rather than its place of origin. The Utrecht Psalter is a rare example of the Carolingian custom of being inspired by classical traditions, but adapting these into something new.

This most valuable book is kept, together with a few other UBU highlights, in the UBU safe. In the new UBU building the special collections will be kept in a depot consisting of various secure and climate-controlled storerooms. One of these storerooms is reserved for manuscripts and rare items, a selection of the oldest and most valuable printed works, a total of several hundred metres of books. In this storeroom there is also a safe where the Utrecht Psalter and several other special manuscripts and rare items are kept: a total of twelve. These rooms are climate-controlled; their temperature varies between 18 and 21°C. As the reading room and the strong room have the same temperature, this will fluctuate slightly with the weather conditions. Humidity is also kept relatively stable: from 50 to 55%.

The Utrecht Psalter is of course rarely lent or even taken out of its storeroom. But when that happens, for an exhibition at the request of a distinguished specialist for example, or – as an unlikely exception, at the request of an important figure like Mary Robinson, at the time the President of Ireland – it will be moved around in the most inconspicuous way possible. No publicity at all will be given to the travels and whereabouts of the Psalter. Recent digitisation of all the pages has made the book highly accessible to the public, while the book itself can stay in its protected environment.

http://vitrine.library.uu.nl/index2.htm (last accessed 26 December 2004). Information from UBU staff

On the Janskerk and Palace of Lodewijk Napoleon

The first building to house the later Utrecht University Library was the choir of the Janskerk. A few years after 1581, when the City of Utrecht had proclaimed the 500-600 books confiscated from monasteries and chapters to be a city library, the canons of St John's offered the choir of their church for use as a city library.

The canons must have thought that this would at least prevent the building from losing too much of its dignity. The City Fathers seized the offer with both hands. The church building did not need to be converted for this new function. Only a room for Cornelis Booth, who became the first librarian in 1640, was built adjacent to the choir. He could work there without losing sight of the library visitors.

The city library – since 1636 the university library – would continue to be housed in the Janskerk for several centuries. Insufficient comfort and lack of facilities in the building would in the end, however, take their toll on the library visitors.

In 1820 the university library moved to the former palace of King Lodewijk Napoleon. He had been appointed King of Holland in 1806 by his brother, the Emperor Napoleon, and had decided to settle in Utrecht. He bought up houses in the block between Drift and Wittevrouwenstraat and commissioned the Amsterdam architect J.D. Zocher Sr. to design a palace here. This was to consist partly of converted canal mansions and partly of new buildings in the interior area and the streets behind. In Zocher's design the buildings enclosed a huge courtyard, which was accessible through Wittevrouwenstraat. The main entrances to the palace and the ballroom were situated on this courtyard.

The palace was already finished in 1809. However, it never became more than a pied-à-terre for Lodewijk Napoleon: on reflection he preferred other palaces like the palace on Dam Square in Amsterdam.

The most spectacular rooms in the palace were the ballroom or grande galerie – a large, elongated space – and the court chapel. Later in the 19th century two galleries, one above the other, were built along the walls in the front part of the ballroom, thus creating different floors. This conversion was also carried out in the other rooms. In 1961 the ballroom was demoted to a book depot. Three floors were made in it using metal grids. The fact that the building subsequently acquired the nickname 'sing-sing' speaks for itself.

The still existing chapel was incorporated by Lodewijk Napoleon into his palace. As part of the library in 1857 the building acquired a steel construction along the walls in order to be able to place bookcases the full height of the walls.

The library complex was extended further as time went by. The administration building with reading rooms and an attractive entrance hall was erected in 1905 on the corner of Wittevrouwenstraat and the present Keizerstraat, with the new book warehouse next door. These buildings would together form the eastern wing of the complex. The courtyard which had been open until then was drastically altered by the building of a pavilion in 1975. The pavilion, meant to be a temporary building for 10 years, filled the greater part of the courtyard. It blocked the existing, clear spatial structure, which meant that while the complex may have gained more space, it also became a disordered whole.

In 2004 the Central Library moved to the new buildings in De Uithof. The Faculty of Languages library continues to be housed in the complex.

Vier eeuwen Universiteitsbibliotheek Utrecht, Utrecht 1986
Onderzoek met betrekking tot de gebouwen van de UBU, Werkplaats voor Architektuur, 2001

...param ni
...la sunt magna.i.
viginti milia qui mei
qui nesciunt homine
et dexteram quod sit in
suam et iumenta multa.
...liquit Ionas prophecia.

Incipit michcas ppha.

Verbum dni quod facm
...en in diebus ioatham
achaz ezechie regu iuda.
quod vidit sup samaria.
...et iherusalem. Audi
populi omnes. et ati

The Zwolle Bible

The Zwolle Bible is one of the highlights of the UBU collection. The six-part Bible was written by hand on parchment and originally contained 125 illuminated initials and border decorations with multicoloured flowering foliage. The books were written in the period from 1464 to 1476 in the House of the Brethren of the Common Life in Zwolle, also known as St. Gregory's House. The illumination was probably done elsewhere. The Zwolle Bible has always attracted much attention, which has meant that a considerable amount of research has been carried out on the six books over the course of time. More is known about them than any other manuscript made in the Netherlands.

The Zwolle Bible is the work of one copyist, Jacobus van Enckhuysen who must have written an average of 22 pages a month out of the total 3400 pages. The work was commissioned by Hermannus Droem who paid 500 golden florins for it, an amount which at that time was enough to buy two stately chapter houses. A large part of the money was spent on the 850 calf hides which were needed for the parchment.

Regrettably the Zwolle Bible is badly damaged. Fifty-two of the illuminated initials have been cut out of the volumes, sometimes with the rest of the page as well. On other pages only the illumination has been removed. One of these was repurchased at a later date and two others can be found in the Museum of the Catharijne Convent in Utrecht. When, in 1995, a fourth initial was put up for auction at Sotheby's in London the UBU was faced with a difficult dilemma: should the asking price of NLG 25.000 (11,350 Euro) be spent on this one 10-by-10-cm. drawing, while the other 50 cut-out initials were still missing from the volumes? In the end the drawing was sold for three times the asking price to an art dealer.

K. van der Horst, 'The long arm of coincidence: the missing initials of the Zwolle Bible', in: Theatrum orbis librorum
Liber amicorum presented to Nico Israel on the occasion of his seventeeth birthday
T. Croiset van Uchelen, K. van der Horst & G. Schilder (eds.). Utrecht 1989, p. 193-223

CITIES OF REFUGE

(Extract from the Tractate Makkoth 10a)

These cities (of refuge) are to be made nei... into... large walled cities, but medium-sized boroughs... established only in the vicinity of a water supply and where there is no water at hand it is to be brought thither; they are to be established only in marketing districts; they are to be established only in populous districts, and if the population has fallen off others are to be brought into the neighbourhood, and if the residents (of any one place) have fallen off, others are brought thither, priests [cohanim], Levites and Israelites. There should be traffic neither in arms nor in trap-gear there: these are the words of R. Nehemiah; but the Sages permit. The... however, agree that no traps may be set there nor may ropes be left dangling about in the place so that the blood avenger may have no occasion to come visiting there.

R. Isaac asked: What is the Scriptural authority (for all these provisions)? - The verse: and that fleeing unto one of these cities he might live (Deuteronomy 4:42) which means - provide him with whatever he needs so that he may [truly] live.

A Tanna taught [a baraitha]: A disciple who goes into banishment is joined in exile by his master, in accordance with the basis of the text: ...that he might live, which means - provide him with whatever he needs so that he may [truly] live. R. Zeira remarked that on the basis of this one might say... let no one reach Maimonides...

Whither are they ban... on the yonder side of... in the land of Canaan... cities beyond the Jord... Canaan; They shall b... cities were selected in... three cities beyond th... ordained, [and of the... cities for refuge shall... that [they did] not [f... simultaneously afford... And direct roads wer... other, as ordained, th... divide the borders of... [ordained] scholar-di... manslayer in case any... way, and that they m... R. Meir says: he may... is ordained, and this i... Judah says: to begin... [one of] the cities of... error or with intent... him thence. Whoever... ...the coun...

Talmud Project

The Talmud Project explores the simultaneous display of multiple related texts.
Several dials allow the reader to trace ideas from one text to another, examine
translations and find text in the larger context of the full corpus.

www.davidsmall.com/projects
(last accessed 10 March 2005)

Previous page:
David Small, The Talmud Project, 2001
Commissioned work for MIT Media Lab, New York

The Internet Archive, Brewster Kahle, a man with a mission, discusses the digital library of the future

'When it comes to libraries, many people cannot see beyond stacks of books. Sometimes I just go crazy. The library world – it just doesn't seem to be moving very fast. The question is, why not? Because I'd say the big opportunity for our generation is that universal access to all knowledge is within our grasp.

The Internet Archive

Let me start with the Internet Archive, an independent non-profit library in San Francisco California. I am an engineer by training and I really wanted to build a library. This was in the late '80s and everybody had been promised a library for a long time. Now either we could scan everything printed or we had to get people to publish on line. It looked like publishing on line was a lot easier. So I helped develop some of the early publishing systems on the Internet. It's an old system that I called WAIS – Wide Area Information Servers. It got a lot of publishers on line. By 1994, that was going well enough for us to say, okay now let's build the library. So in 1996 we started the Internet Archive and also the Alexis Internet, which is cataloguing the web, trying to do traditional cataloguing. But how do you do that to the size of the web? We just started sucking down the whole web and tried putting a catalogue on top. Instead of taking the library and moving towards the web - it's taking the web and building a library out of it. A very different and interesting approach. And it's large. It just comes in huge quantities. Around this time, Raj Reddy from Carnegie Melon said, "Let's digitalize a million books!" He then got the Indian and the Chinese government to agree to do all the scanning if the United States would supply the books and scanners. They saw this as a pretty good deal since they would acquire literally tons of new digitalized books for the cost of photocopying a book. To our surprise, the American libraries wouldn't lend us the books; they were worried about not getting them back. So we bought a hundred thousand books, packed up 80 tons of them in four containers and shipped them off. We tried to select material from libraries that was good but not the stuff that should be bowed down to. Plenty of people are taking care of the really nice works. We were trying to make sure all the rest of it was there cost efficiently.

What I find fascinating is to make all the published works of humankind available. From Sumerian tablets onwards; all books, all music, all video, all software, all web pages. That's where we start. That's not necessarily all knowledge, it's not everything that's passed from one generation to another. But it's a pretty good start.

Books

Take books for instance. The total number of books in the largest print library in the world, which is the Library of Congress, is 26 million books. For the Universe of all Books, multiply it by something. It has been estimated that there are 100 million books ever. An average book, if you had it in a word processor format, would be about a megabyte in size. 26 million megabytes is 26 terabytes. 26 terabytes fits in a bookshelf that would be underneath this desk. And it costs about $60,000. So for the cost of a small house one could have a stored copy of all the words in the Library of Congress. All on hard drives, so it could be serving that to tens of thousands, hundreds of thousands of people. Digitizing a book as best we can tell from our experience working with India and China, if you are efficient about it, is about $10.00 a book. You'd spend more on the Gutenberg Bible, but most books aren't. If you want to make an image of every page of an average size book and put it through optical character recognition so you could search it, it will cost about $10.00. So if we take the Library of Congress again of 26 million books that's 260 million dollars, which is half of their budget for one year and it's a tiny fraction (a little over 1%) of the amount the United States spends every year on libraries. And then we'd have the whole Library of Congress digitized.

Music

So books are possible to do. Music is a little harder. It looks like there are 2-3 million audio recordings that have been published in the last century. We're starting to have these materials digitized, from wax drum recordings and 78s and LPs. It takes more than just a bookshelf under the table, but we're still talking within amounts of money that are perfectly reasonable to get these materials stored. It's within our grasp. 2-3 million objects are not that many. Then we need to find solutions to make them widely available; some for a fee, some for free. There are people who are trying to promote the idea of compulsory licenses, like on radio. But for now, let's at least put the public domain on line.

Movies and Television

Then there are movies. There are 100-200 thousand theatrical releases of movies. The kind of material you'd think of as Hollywood feature films, half of which are from India. We have a huge collection of these. But there are also ephemeral films that weren't meant for the ages but are often really wonderful documentary records of what came before. We're in the process of digitizing large numbers of these and making them available. We're also showing how archives can do it for themselves or how we can help them do it. It turns out it's very inexpensive to digitize these types of materials. We've also spun off a business to do this; actually we've already spun off four businesses in the last two years to basically handle the digitization and storage of these materials and other industries to work with libraries.

It is very pro-capitalist work that we're doing. The idea is to make these things more available so people can use them for all sorts of things. Television has been estimated as being about 400 channels of original TV around the world. The TV archive has started archiving about 20 channels of this 24 hours a day DVD quality about five years ago. It's a large amount of material but it's still something a small organization can do. At least it's being preserved.

The Wayback Machine

In 1996 we also started the Wayback Machine, archiving all publicly available websites. We took a snapshot every two months and continue now to do so. Basically we're trying to record everything so people can surf the web as it was.

As George Orwell put it, 'those who control the past control the present. Those who control the present control the future'. So if there is no record of the past that is accessible to people, it's as if it has been erased. And people can make up whatever they said they said. This doesn't make any sense in an open society. So we are recording the web and then making it available as widely as we can through the Wayback Machine. It's a free service on archive.org.

You can type in a URL and see past versions of websites. It's a collection that is growing at 20 terabytes a month, that's about the size of the Library of Congress. Hundreds of thousands of people use it every day. It now gets about 100 requests a second. So the Wayback Machine is fairly popular in terms of being able to provide enduring access to materials that are often removed from the web for all sorts of reasons. The average lifetime of a web page is only 100 days, but these are often great works. They are works of tens of millions of people that belong in the library. So you can see things, search over time; see how the usage of terms have changed over the years. It's fantastic not only to search to find documents but also to see trends. The advent of the archive will pave the way for all sorts of interesting search technologies.

The Internet Archive Collections: San Francisco, Alexandria, Amsterdam

Of course we have to make sure that these materials survive and not just get destroyed in circumstances. The history of libraries is that they are burned by those in power at the time... sometimes by accident but usually on purpose. In the book world there are and were copies in multiple places. That's why we still have so many great works even though the Library of Alexandria burned. But often in the digital world often there's only one copy and it rests with the publisher. So our idea is to make digital libraries with copies of these materials in multiple places. We made a copy of everything we had in San Francisco and gave it to the new Library of Alexandria in Egypt. Now we're building a library in Amsterdam in the Netherlands to serve the European community. It will be a European archive that will collect things that are important to the European Union countries. These things also replicate those in other places so that as time goes along and disasters occur, we can prevent losing things as we have so dramatically in the past.

The Internet and the Public Domain

Nowadays all human knowledge can be made available to everyone no matter where they are in the world because storage technology and computer networks like the Internet. The question is: do we as a society want it? People can obstruct it for political reasons, copyright reasons, ego reasons, for institutional exclusivity and so on. Or are we actually going to live in an open society? I'm putting my effort behind an open society. At the moment, the concept of the public library system is being thwarted. Because of new copyright regulations the balance gets out of skew. The concept of what a public domain, or a commons, or what intellectual discourse is for, is really changing in our consumer times. I think maybe we can learn something from the way it was done for hundreds of years rather than what happened in the last thirty or forty years with the rise of major corporate ownership. There have been some changes recently that are making it much more difficult for our children to have access to the great works of humankind.

But we hope the wisdom that spawned the idea of pubic libraries survives the current corporate age. The library can now encompass more than just those who can get through the publishing systems via digitalization and the Internet.

It's the people's medium.

It's the people's library.

Based on conversations with Brewster Kahle in July 2003 and June 2004.
Gerard Baltussen, Marijke Beek, Eva DeCarlo and Bas Savenije.

Internet Archive Wayback Machine
www.archive.org/web/web.php
(last accessed 10 March 2005)

A Library of Spatial Manuscripts
The Vedute Foundation

Vedute was founded in 1991 with the purpose of building up a collection of spatial manuscripts: a 'library' of visualised thoughts that make the concept of space accessible and tangible. The concept of space in the size of a book.
§Vedute invites designers, architects, artists and others active in different disciplines to visualise their personal view on the notion of space in a work measuring 44 x 32 x 7 cm in a closed form. The dimensions are derived from those of a book, but unlike books, the 3-D manuscripts reveal their content as visual statements. Some are directly accessible; others reveal their content step by step.

Some manuscripts were acquired individually; others are part of one of the theme projects Vedute has initiated, such as The City Library of the Senses (1995), '00:00 Time & Duality' (1999-2000), Acoustic Architecture-Architecture Acoustics (1999-2000) and Vedute in Rotterdam, Rotterdam in Vedute (2004). Vedute aims to give new impetus to the debate about space and architecture, by regularly showing parts of the collection.

The collection has been growing rapidly over time. The library as a whole now contains 154 pieces.

The Vedute collection has for years led a relatively wandering existence which means that works have been exhibited in various places, and in various cities and countries.

The Vedute collection has now found a new, permanent, home in the Netherlands Architecture Institute in Rotterdam.

Views on Vedute, brochure Stichting Vedute, May 1996
Stichting Vedute www.vedute.nl/about.html
(last accessed 10 March 2005)

IN THE LIBRARY

As I have moved from city to city, the local public or university library has always been a place I could rely on. That is where the writer finds readers interested in his work, and if he has some free time, he settles down off towards the window behind the ramparts of books he has pulled off the shelves in his curiosity. I have always been particularly intrigued by hidden, out-of-the-way, little-known libraries that are less attractive to the larger public: their smell and gloomy shadows are unmistakable – and even the motes of dust dancing through their sunbeams spell out the tiny letters of some secret runes. By paying a visit to other authors, he returns to himself and his own domains of thought, taking up again the unceasing silent dialogue he pursues with the speakers of other truths who pop up in all kinds of masks and ask him to dance, which can lead either to closeness or greater distance. I have had the feeling in a great many libraries that I could easily remain there forever, but nonetheless have always ended up fleeing sooner or later. This is the place where the author sees himself on the shelves, with all the portraits of him in earlier days, bound up, the successes and failures alike. He is the same as the shelf that bears his books, side by side with his colleagues, living and dead, whose names start with the same letters.

That is what he is, or has become. His years stand in a row, years in which he has played a number of figures. And if the author manages to free himself from such unfitting attention focused on his own books, he gladly chats with the librarians, whose knowledge is sometimes frightening. Amid the vast panorama, the jungle of catalogues, his own lonely name becomes slimmer and slimmer, until it is finally all but unnoticeable.

People do not generally horse around in libraries, or kick up much of a ruckus; here even the wildest are made lambs, and the librarian metes out to all her strictest gaze, disapproving of even the faintest whisper. She is a priestess after all, prescribing with a raising of her brows behavior befitting the holiness of books.

I recall a joint conference of librarians from the Netherlands and Hungary in the early nineties. The Dutch ambassador had finished his opening speech in the marble-columned aula of the National Library (formerly the royal palace) in Buda. Mine was to follow.

I expressed my happiness that the fading letter "Z," once stamped on entries for editions of my books in many languages, no longer had any meaning. Before 1989, this had indicated that the book in question was considered "Closed Material," requiring special permission to read it. The librarians were less interested in this topic than in the new perspectives being opened up the introduction of information technology, which seemed to be the unanimous orientation of the younger attendees.

It must be a generational issue, given that both the Ambassador and I were emotionally devoted to books: you can pick them up (or even paw them) with your hands, open and close them; they have color and smell, and they do not flicker.

In a word, they have a sensual existence. (Still, we were perfectly happy about the Dutch-Hungarian collaboration in Information Technology.) We spoke somewhat defensively, as if carrying the flag for the old men, pursuing the shelter of respect for the book as a work of art, given its special qualities. Still, let me mention the remark of Sigfried Unseld, the Great German publisher who passed away last year, regarding Marshall McLuhan's prophecy of impending death for the Gutenberg Galaxy: he noted that, three decades on, two things had changed: McLuhan had died and the number of his books in print had multiplied many times over.

If I painted the portrait of a humanistic scholar, I would like to see barely-negotiable towers of books rising up around the subject, organized according to some mysterious system. Whenever I have met with professors in a departmental library, I was always quite moved as I departed, thinking these excellent people were in their proper place, undoubtedly passing beautiful days there in their cave.

In the old-style departmental libraries, books obtained on interlibrary loan accumulated in worrisome heaps around the scholar. A friend of mine became so attached to them that he insisted on having them around always, which resulted in some unpleasant administrative correspondence.

But it will be a terrible loss for humankind if this image of the bookworm becomes an old-fashioned oddity. Whatever the case, I would also gladly preserve another image, that of my Latin teacher, who spent his free hours in the faculty library – at the top of the ladder, to be exact. He could step it sideways as dexterously as a house painter. When I asked him what a true philologist was like, he immediately replied that this was one who read constantly if he could. There was a sofa in the library where my teacher would sleep if his wife did not come for him, because, he said with the smile of one sitting on a secret, there is nothing better than early-morning reading.

I quickly became aware of the cautious and tactful ties between researcher and librarian, when the latter notices that indeed, this one here is reading something interesting, looking for the sources of some original thought. The more rarely-touched the book requested by the reader, the higher he rises in the librarian's eyes. But he in turn finds something of interest in the ladies running the library who have had a look into so many books, one just as good as the next; the book-wonders flow in a long line. They feel the library to be greater than the sum of its books.

The soul of the librarian experiences a mixture of respect and pity when looking on the fierce reader, sensing that this one, say, is no great dancer, nor too dazzling on the tennis court either, and that maybe the girls are not necessarily dying to have dinner with him, or go on day-trips. I am content to envision the image of the now-deceased director of the Rabbinical Seminary, Sándor Scheiber, in the library of that academy, whose chaotic state represented a special kind of permanence. I see him slanted to the right, leaning on his elbow in a bottomed-out armchair amid a mass of books, where he also worked on the side as an artist of matchmaking, recommending the right girl to the right boy. Though he and I had a good relationship, he once pulled my future wife aside and counseled her against me.

The Head Rabbi was an accomplished philologist and Talmudist. I once asked him whether he thought it possible for a true scholar of the Talmud, upon seeing a pin pushed through its pages, could tell all the letters the pin passed through, based on its entry point on the front page. The rabbi, after considerable thought, said he thought it possible, as long as the pin went in straight.

These were cool, stone-floored halls, whose air was gentle and wooden stairs creaky, and reading rooms whose floors were waxed. Down the strip of carpet on the stairs would come the librarians on tiptoe; their hips assumed an even more advantageous roundness from this gait.

There was a constancy in that silence, in those rustlings, in those women and men in smocks who would catalogue items, reading a little from each one, then catalogue some more. Some would retain every last book in their minds, suffering as a result but unable to expunge some bits of text on the most horrific subjects they had no more than glanced at.

I can see before me the old-style catalogue cases on casters that bore the traces of so many ancient hands of gentle curlicues.

Generations of amateurs brought their collections together in an old school or city library. From time to time, harsh danger would threaten: armies would come and – a pleasant surprise – would set guards in front of the library, given the danger of some coming in drunk, feeling the cold, and making a fire there.

Floods might also come and wash the books off downriver towards the sea.

You could also rightfully fear that the planes of one of Europe's culture-loving countries might drop a bomb on it, not really aiming, just out for some collateral destruction. The irreplaceables are destroyed again, as they so often are.

After the war, ex libris seals from family libraries started appearing in the libraries of the city. Personal libraries suffer all sorts of fates, but there are among them a lucky few, museum-pieces, or the collections of cloisters or magnates, that come through unscathed. Some are complete like this, with no need for any expansion: the books, taken together, form an ultimately perfect work.

I used to like looking at the Danube from the windows of the libraries in the Parliament and the Hungarian Academy; imagination flowed with the river out from the constancy of the stone embankment. Sometimes the library gives us the impulse to flee, persecuted by our ignorance and pursued by what we do not know; we would rather run off to see the girls, or to some happy gathering. Others have written too much already. In fact, everything has been written. Why throw another book on the pile?

Well, because that is the best life there is. It is the envy of schoolchildren, who still love reading and want to continue it their whole lives through. You get a special feeling sitting in an enormous reading room, getting inspiration from the heads you see in the halo of each lamp, students at exam time whose intelligent foreheads occasionally slump down onto their book.

They take the snack they have packed to the room in front of the snack bar, or out to the bank of the Danube to stroll up and down.

A boy spots a girl in the reading room, one he has not seen in his immediate circle at the university.

He looks at her. She notices this, and steals a look or two at him. When their eyes meet, they both blush. (It helps to have a despicable librarian, since then they can exchange conspiratorial glances.) Of course we are always curious what the other is reading. Oh, that! He (or she) must be so interesting!

So the fellow reader now has a legitimate excuse to slide a slip of paper to the girl or boy in question. A date follows soon afterward, a rendezvous in the lounge, or under the arcade.

These events have their precursors: observation of her pen, or notebook, or her hands, or the straight (or twisted) way she holds her mouth, perhaps her smell, and what sort of grimaces she pulls at the things she is reading, what a lively internal discourse she is having with the book's author.

There are some library users who practically live in the reading room. There they emit all sorts of vapors into the shared atmosphere. Their reading can be bizarrely quirky. Some are builders: you can practically see their thoughts as they move forward step by step. You can ask them a question during a break, drawn not by amatory interest but by curiosity and thirst for knowledge. I became friends with a man who regularly plucked the Nouvelle Revue Française off the shelf from under my nose. It was always an interesting exercise to divine the intellectual character of those around us at the table based on the books they requested, stealing peeks at their spines. The eccentrics, the scholars, the philologists, the students at Party schools – all were easily identified by their reading, and how much time they spent at it, and what languages they read in.

The guessing game was to figure out why they were there. Perhaps preparing for an exam, or aiming to qualify for a raise in pay? Or simple insatiability of interest grabbing onto the requisite, enlightening text – the hungry predator seizing its prey? You could distinguish between the common, the original, and the eccentric mind. The library is a mixture of shared existence and far-reaching individuality. I am one with my readings, building of them a complete virtual world. Why I move on from one book to another, and what kind of honey (or poison) I sip from them, is my own secret, impenetrable to the reader sitting beside me. Physical proximity, separation of mind.

It was wonderful to sit in the Great Hall of Reading – the training room of concentration – with the absorption characteristic of church. Your physical being is pushed off into the background, while your mind focuses in on the subject at hand.

This is the zone where it is not impolite to speak to an author. Here both reader and writer are on the same side – people of the book – across from the opposite shore where non-readers gather. The river is the stream of books; the letters pour by. At this very moment, millions of people are writing.

The library is a major workshop in the factory that turns out a society. It deserves to be placed in the center of the city. This is, after all, where the brains tend to gather; it towers high over all other public buildings against thought's sky. It would be appropriate for people passing by it to doff their hats, or at least give a nod.

There are alliances within the library as well, all manner of theoretical revolutionaries ready to play their parts when the day of action comes, studying the authors picked out by the brain trust for their strategy.

Another wonderful moment: when we spot one of the true, great scholars, watching to see how he takes his notes, with what, in what sort of notebook, what kind of faces he makes while doing it. Does he ever lift his head? Give dismissive flicks of a finger?

It is a bonus to have a view of a nice oak tree out the window, or a great river, or an exciting square: fertile contrast between inside and out. What you see when you raise your eyes is an important part of the experience.

We can see the trackers whom one book leads on to another. The interested reader is helped onward on his path of research by debate, by simple mention, and by praise and invective.

The state and consistency of a library provides a precise characterization of a given country's political system. What it chooses, what it retains, and what it sets out in the reference room – these things say a lot about the openness and intellectual character of a city.

When the private lending libraries were closed or taken over by the state, and prohibited books removed from the public libraries were placed in closed warehouses or taken to the mulching machines, I was very precise in noting what books could be borrowed where. It was a great moment when my teacher suggested I borrow whatever I liked from his personal library, opening the doors of the glass cabinet. Even the teacher became a private individual when reading, like the student, since we are all students in the face of the great books.

Readers of more powerful imagination can see the author in their mind's eye, shoes, lapel and all. They see the hair on head and face that go along with the mind.

I would call my fellow readers' attention to a particularly interesting paragraph with a faint pencil line along the edge of the page.

There is drama in the library as well: someone falls off his chair, or someone's shoulder is touched by the librarian, or someone is expected outside, and two strapping men take him by the arms.

People allow themselves breaks of various duration to chat. In the days when we still smoked, a cigarette was a good excuse to step out.

I just want to finish this book before closing time, or pick it up tomorrow in the same place, on page one-sixty eight. We sense the librarians' impatience for us to get up and return the books a quarter-hour before closing at the latest.

Once we have sated ourselves on authors, and experienced the marvel of greatness, then we are drawn again by our everyday human experiences and proportions. To stroll arm in arm after the cool breezes of the intellect felt good beyond description. Libraries and books inspire strolls together, and walking another home, and sometimes marriage.

I found good use in going to the library instead of class. It would have been even better had I been able to turn without inhibition to a widely-read library representative who could understand and empathize with the nature of my curiosity, helping me on my way with a few productive suggestions. Such librarians are like good family doctors: they know a book for every problem. Even if it does not entirely solve it, at least it illuminates, and helps us see more clearly.

I am drawn to energetic contrasting pairs of long, pendulous swings. For example, I like to imagine the library as a little nook or magical place of refuge, with the book as sensual pleasure (sight, touch, smell) that vaporizes into an intangible mist, creating some kind of impression of the work in our minds and hearts. (I would like to know that the word heart still has currency in global information technology circles – though any ordinary catheterization can show us our on a monitor, with all the traffic flowing inside it. Though we cannot put our finger on the hidden feelings inside it, still such a short word carries an almost endless significance as an image that it cannot go out of fashion. Its use is thoroughly justified.) So here I return to the fundamental antinomy of the intimate worlds of heart and mind on the one hand, and fabulous world-libraries on the other – we read ever more frequently that such things are in the making – that owe their existence to the far-reaching achievements of digitalization. We read of projects, of practical utopians pulling together all of human knowledge; if we take this thread even farther, we can imagine that the whole trove of human intelligence will be transplanted to the moon, or some other celestial body, in a clever receptacle for ensured survival should some tragedy befall the earth, allowing us to pass on our common essence, so to speak, to other intelligent beings, in the form of the vast corpus of written texts.

How marvelous it is that the contents of libraries give an unprejudiced picture of the essence of humanity. As long as we are talking about texts, or knowledge that can be transmitted through books, the librarian can tell you straight out what books in the library should be considered, since each contains a mixture of wisdom and stupidity. So the responsibility of posthumous selection is thereby passed on to mysterious scholars who – somewhere, somehow – will devote time to earth's past millennia, if they are in the mood. If such all-encompassing storehouses of memory are possible, then their mere existence justifies the opposite pole, the justification for individual reading. All the more so, since the book is a fairly reliable object, while electronically stored texts tend to disappear in a relatively short span of time, and the machines and programs that read magnetic information will disappear at a similar pace. Futuristic talk of the end of the age of paper and a reliability of electronic signals surpassing the Gutenberg Galaxy – this is simple-minded bombast. "Quick" and "lasting" are not synonyms. Circumspect, thorough preservation of texts does not renounce any form of storage. If possible, such an approach would not just write worthy sentences on paper or parchment, but also carve them into stone.

It has become more frequent, and hence more natural, to switch off between these two poles, and pit them against one another in dialectic opposition, the realm of the individual and of humanity as a whole. This pendulum of thought swings right through any intermediate dividing walls or distinctions set up by the human race. The universal and individual perspectives do not conflict; universal history and one-time narrative reinforce one another.

The engineer working on storing all existing books digitally likes to read real books under the intimate halo of his lampshade. When Bill Gates was asked what he liked to write with, he raised his fountain pen.

The tanÿble and intanÿble are not enemies, nor are the sensual and the intellectual. A writer, whose profession requires him to be receptive to ambiguities and paradoxes, cannot espouse one pole at the expense of the other.

Let digitalization (thank God for its successes!) take ever greater bites out of the store of knowledge; this very progress only increases desire for the private, the banal, the personal, the intimate – for person-to-person experiences and dialogues.

The more universal we become, the more distinctive each of us gets at the same time. To take this thought further, I prefer small libraries to large ones. Street-corner libraries, outfitted with cafés or teahouses, a well-planned layout encompassing areas for reading and for discussion also – a place to stop in if we have a little free time and are in the mood for shared solitude, or solitary companionship, so characteristic of modern metropolis-dwellers.

I can conceive of such corner libraries becoming meeting places that serve many functions. In books we find the remedy for neglected loneliness and all manner of spiritual sadness, as long as someone offers us a welcoming place to sit, and puts just the right book into our hands.

I know how important books must be for those in prison, to keep them from being entirely cut off from the human race. It is only logical that the librarian is also a doctor and social worker at the same time.

Having grown up in Debrecen, one of Hungary's outlying cities, I have my teacher there at the Calvinist Gimnázium, and its librarian, to thank for my introduction to world literature from the age of fourteen. I have never regretted making a life out of the word, being a lover of it and the varied associations it can string together. The dedication of the new university library at Utrecht, and your kind invitation, allow me to express my grateful appreciation for the profession – and the calling – of the librarian.

György Konrád

This text was written especially for the book Living Library and read by György Konrád at the official opening of the UBU on 17 March, 2005.

shh!

'At first we were sceptical about mobile phones in the library, Bas Savenije mentioned to us. We knew that students always want to be reachable at all times and if we didn't allow their telephones, they probably wouldn't visit the library. So we let the students leave their phones on and after an initial observance we found that it was not a disturbance to anyone.'

Previous page:
Cartoon mocking the accessibility of books
at the UBU before the galleries were added.
Students Almanac Mutua Fides, 1875

BIBLIOTHECÆ
TRAIECTINÆ
CATALOGVS.

(handwritten note, partly legible):
In Catalogum Bibliothecæ Trajectinæ, ad ... ejus bi... Bibliotheca, et Acad... ... Urbisq; Celeberrim... ... Nobilissim... Magnificis Magi... Trajectinæ ... æternam memo... honorem, ... quam æternum m... ... habebit is... Musarum Patronus ... procurandum, dono dat Bibliothecæ Assurgentis ... cui per ... augmentum ... Christianus Ravius Berlin... Trajecti ad Rhenum, Anno 1645 mense Julio.

TYPIS SALOMONIS RHODII,

Anno cIɔ.Iɔ.cIIX.

Catalogues

The first catalogue of the UBU, at that time still the City library, was not arranged alphabetically by author as was customary later, but systematically according to subject. Theological, legal, medical, historical, philosophical and literary works were described according to field and then ordered within each field by language and size. As far as we know, the first Utrecht catalogue, which appeared in 1608, was the first in the Netherlands to give practical information about the collection and the library itself in the national language rather than just in Latin. The language of each book is indicated by the typeface used: titles of works written in Latin are set in roman characters, Romance languages in italics, and German texts in Gothic lettering. Thanks to this catalogue the fame of the UBU spread for the first time far beyond the boundaries of the city and the country.

In 1664 a new, more user-friendly catalogue appeared which for the first time also mentioned the posi,tion numbers of the books. The division according to language had been dropped and books were distinguished instead by their size. Books of each size were then sorted according to subject and after that alphabetically according to author or 'headword'. After 1664 a few more catalogues were published, but the first, completely alphabetical catalogue of the UBU appeared in 1834. In the two volumes each book is described in detail and also for the first time a proper alphabetical catalogue is made.

Around 1860 another more flexible and less costly system of cataloguing, copied from Leiden University library, was introduced in Utrecht. In a loose-leaf system of catalogue booklets, called the Leiden booklets, titles were printed on index cards together and also what were referred to as 'multiples' and 'references'. Recent acquisitions could be inserted by hand. This job was carried out weekly until 1980, so that users of the library had up-to-date access to the collection. At that time there were about half a million title descriptions and a total of more than one million index cards.

These Leiden booklets were then entered one by one into the computer. At the end of 2004 this work had still not been completed; the majority of the collection of 9554 Leiden booklets is kept in the new library building in one of the depots. Those which have not yet been entered in the computer catalogue are still available for consultation by users and will be digitised in the coming years.

Vier eeuwen Universiteitsbibliotheek Utrecht, Utrecht 1986, pp. 49-54, 76-79, 176-177, 225-226
Information UBU staff members

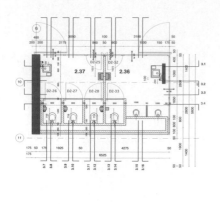

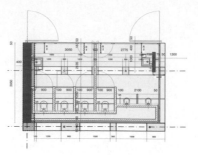

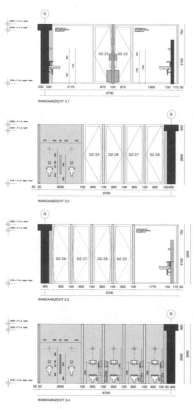

WANDAANZICHT 3.1

WANDAANZICHT 3.2

WANDAANZICHT 3.3

WANDAANZICHT 3.4

WANDAANZICHT 3.5 vervallen

WANDAANZICHT 3.6 vervallen

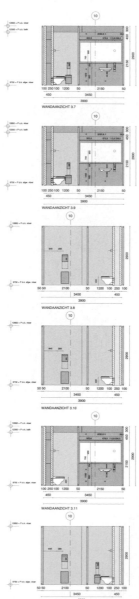

WANDAANZICHT 3.7

WANDAANZICHT 3.9

WANDAANZICHT 3.8

WANDAANZICHT 3.10

WANDAANZICHT 3.11

WANDAANZICHT 3.12

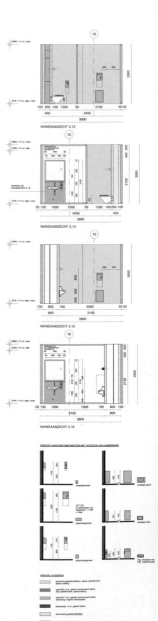

WANDAANZICHT 3.13

WANDAANZICHT 3.14

WANDAANZICHT 3.15

WANDAANZICHT 3.16

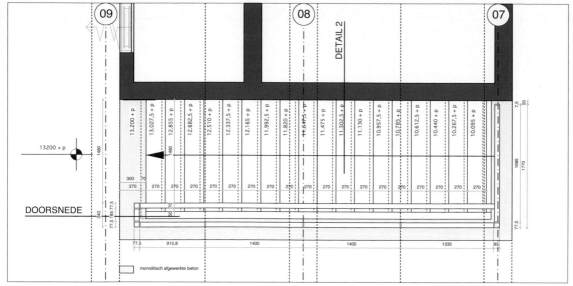

PLATTEGROND 3E VERDIEPING

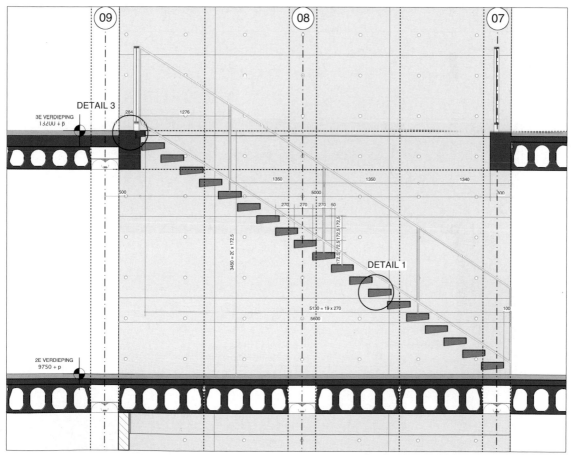

DOORSNEDE

2200

960

200

000

doorsnede naar werkplekken

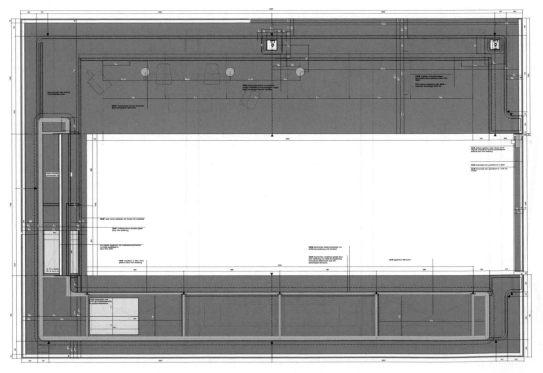

bovenaanzicht

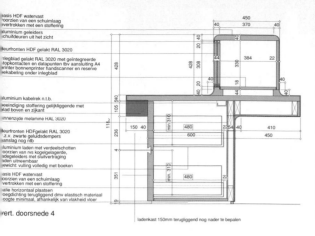

basis HDF watervast
voorzien van een schuimlaag
overtrokken met een stoffering

aluminium geleiders
schuifdeuren uit het zicht

kleurfronten HDF gelakt RAL 3020

inlegblad gelakt RAL 3020 met geïntegreerde
stopkontacten en datapunten tbv aansluiting A4
printer bonnenprinter handscanner en reserve
bekabeling onder inlegblad

aluminium kabelrek n.t.b.

beeindiging stoffering gelijkliggende met
blad boven en zijkant

binnenzijde melamine HAL 3020

kleurfronten HDFgelakt RAL 3020
z.v. zwarte geluidsdempers
aanslag nog ntb

aluminium laden met verdeelschotten
voorzien van rvs kogelgelagerde,
ladegeleiders met sluitvertraging
laden uitneembaar
gewicht: vulling volledig met boeken

basis HDF watervast
voorzien van een schuimlaag
overtrokken met een stoffering

balie horizontaal plaatsen
voegdichting terugliggend dmv elastisch materiaal
hoogte minimaal, afhankelijk van vlakheid van vloer

vert. doorsnede 4

ladenkast 150mm terugliggend nog nader te bepalen

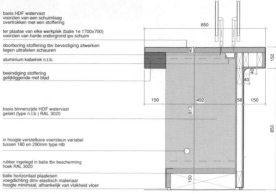

basis HDF watervast
voorzien van een schuimlaag
overtrokken met een stoffering

ter plaatse van elke werkplek (balie 1e 1700x700)
voorzien van harde ondergrond ipv schuim

doorboring stoffering tbv bevestiging afwerken
tegen uitrafelen scheuren

aluminium kabelrek n.t.b.

beeindiging stoffering
gelijkliggende met blad

basis binnenzijde HDF watervast
gelakt (type n.t.b.) RAL 3020

in hoogte verstelbare voersteun variabel
tussen 180 en 290mm type ntb

rubber ingelegd in balie tbv bescherming
hoek RAL 3020

balie horizontaal plaatesen
voegdichting dmv elastisch materiaal
hoogte minimaal, afhankelijk van vlakheid van vloer

vert. doorsnede 1

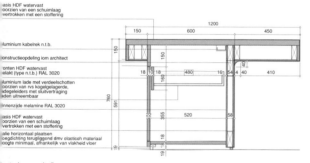

basis HDF watervast
voorzien van een schuimlaag
overtrokken met een stoffering

aluminium kabelrek n.t.b.

constructieopdeling iom architect

fronten HDF watervast
gelakt (type n.t.b.) RAL 3020

aluminium lade met verdeelschotten
voorzien van rvs kogelgelagerde,
ladegeleiders met sluitvertraging
laden uitneembaar

binnenzijde melamine RAL 3020

basis HDF watervast
voorzien van een schuimlaag
overtrokken met een stoffering

balie horizontaal plaatsen
voegdichting terugliggend dmv elastisch materiaal
hoogte minimaal, afhankelijk van vlakheid vloer

vert. doorsnede 5

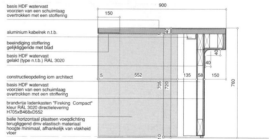

basis HDF watervast
voorzien van een schuimlaag
overtrokken met een stoffering

ter plaatse van elke werkplek en raadpleegplek
voorzien van harde ondergrond ipv schuim

aluminium kabelrek n.t.b.

beeindiging stoffering
gelijkliggende met blad

basis HDF watervast
gelakt (type n.t.b.) RAL 3020

constructieopdeling iom architect

basis HDF watervast
voorzien van een schuimlaag
overtrokken met een stoffering

balie horizontaal plaatesen
voegdichting dmv elastisch materiaal
hoogte minimaal, afhankelijk van vlakheid vloer

vert. doorsnede 3

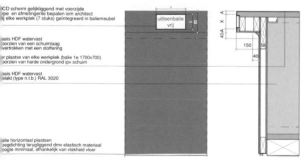

LCD scherm gelijkliggend met voorzijde
type en afmetingerte bepalen iom architect
elk werkplek (7 stuks) geïntegreerd in baliemeubel

uitleenbalie
vrij

basis HDF watervast
voorzien van een schuimlaag
overtrokken met een stoffering

ter plaatse van elke werkplek (balie 1e 1700x700)
voorzien van harde ondergrond ipv schuim

basis HDF watervast
gelakt (type n.t.b.) RAL 3020

balie horizontaal plaatsen
voegdichting terugliggend dmv elastisch materiaal
hoogte minimaal, afhankelijk van vlakheid vloer

vert. doorsnede 2

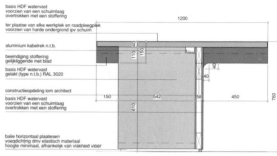

basis HDF watervast
voorzien van een schuimlaag
overtrokken met een stoffering

aluminium kabelrek n.t.b.

beeindiging stoffering
gelijkliggende met blad

basis HDF watervast
gelakt (type n.t.b.) RAL 3020

constructieopdeling iom architect

basis HDF watervast
voorzien van een schuimlaag
overtrokken met een stoffering

brandvrije ladenkasten "Fireking Compact"
kleur RAL 3020 directielevering
H705xB468xD552

balie horizontaal plaatsen voegdichting
terugliggend dmv elastisch materiaal
hoogte minimaal, afhankelijk van vlakheid
vloer

vert. doorsnede 6

gelakt type ntb

stoffering ntb

opmerkingen algermeen

- de opdelingen van de baliekomponenten dienen in overleg met de architect bepaalt worden
- de opdelingen zijn na plaatsing niet meer zichtbaar
- stiknaden iom architect te bepalen
- binnenzijde corpus en laden melamine in ntb kleur
- constructie balie uit te werken door interieurbouwer iom architect

---

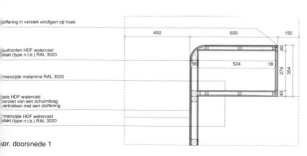

stoffering in verstek eindigen op hoek

kleurfronten HDF watervast
gelakt (type n.t.b.) RAL 3020

binnenzijde melamine RAL 3020

basis HDF watervast
voorzien van een schuimlaag
overtrokken met een stoffering

binnenzijde HDF watervast
gelakt (type n.t.b.) RAL 3020

hor. doorsnede 1

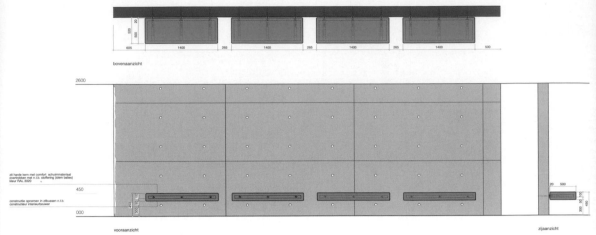

bovenaanzicht

2600

zit harde kern met comfort schuimmateriaal
overtrokken met n.t.b. stoffering (idem balies)
kleur RAL 3020

450

constructie opnemen in zitkussen n.t.b.
constructeur interieurbouwer

000

vooraanzicht

zijaanzicht

wand entreegebied 4 zitelementen tegen muur

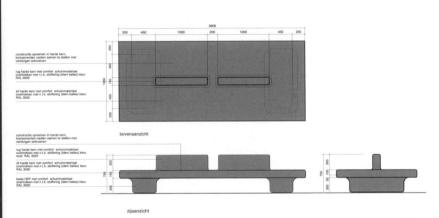

3600

constructie opnemen in harde kern,
komponenten nadien samen te stellen met
verborgen schroeven

rug harde kern met comfort schuimmateriaal
overtrokken met n.t.b. stoffering (idem balies) kleur
RAL 3020

zit harde kern met comfort schuimmateriaal
overtrokken met n.t.b. stoffering (idem balies) kleur
RAL 3020

bovenaanzicht

constructie opnemen in harde kern,
komponenten nadien samen te stellen met
verborgen schroeven

rug harde kern met comfort schuimmateriaal
overtrokken met n.t.b. stoffering (idem balies) kleur
rood RAL 3020

zit harde kern met comfort schuimmateriaal
overtrokken met n.t.b. stoffering (idem balies) kleur
RAL 3020

basis HDF met comfort schuimmateriaal
overtrokken met n.t.b. stoffering (idem balies)
kleur RAL 3020

zijaanzicht

zitbedden 5 stuks

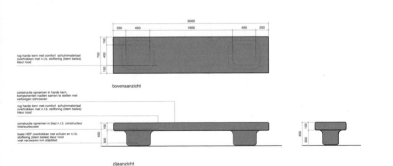

3000

rug harde kern met comfort schuimmateriaal
overtrokken met n.t.b. stoffering (idem balies)
kleur rood

bovenaanzicht

constructie opnemen in harde kern,
komponenten nadien samen te stellen met
verborgen schroeven

rug harde kern met comfort schuimmateriaal
overtrokken met n.t.b. stoffering (idem balies)
kleur rood

constructie opnemen in blad n.t.b. constructeur
interieurbouwer

basis HDF overtrokken met schuim en n.t.b.
stoffering (idem balies) kleur rood
voet verzwaren ivm stabiliteit

zijaanzicht

zitbanken 17 stuks

stoffering ntb

opmerkingen algemeen

- de opdelingen van de baliekomponenten dienen in overleg met de architect bepaalt worden
- de opdelingen zijn na plaatsing niet meer zichtbaar
- stiknaden iom architect te bepalen
- binnenzijde corpus en laden melamine in ntb kleur
- constructie uit te werken door interieurbouwer iom arvhitect

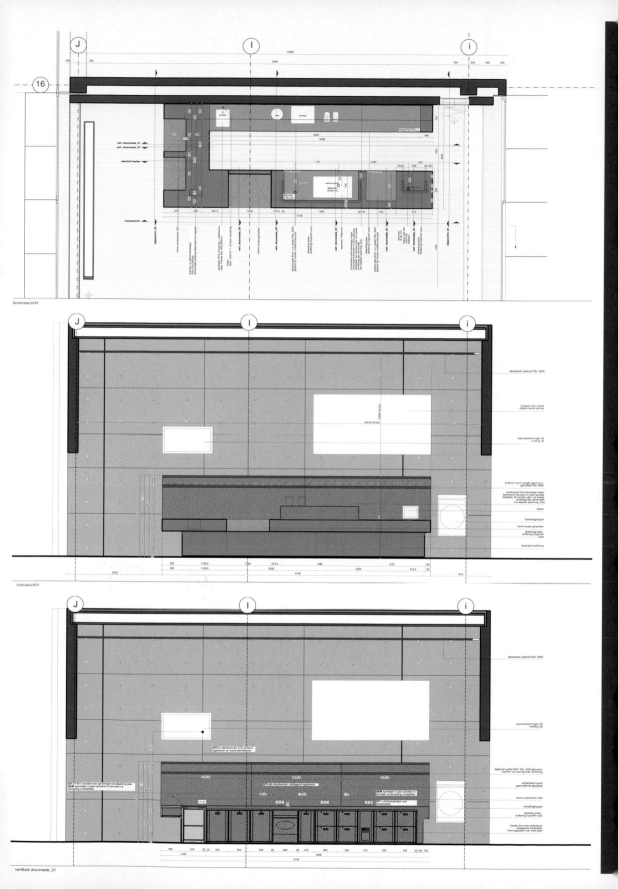

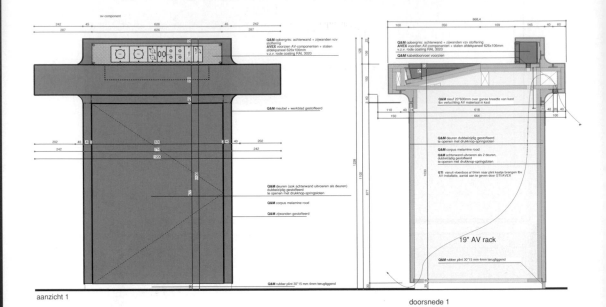

sv-component

Q&M opbergnis: achterwand + zijwanden vzv stoffering
AVEX voorzien AV-componenten + stalen afdekpaneel 626x106mm
v.z.v. rode coating RAL 3020

Q&M meubel + werkblad gestoffeerd

Q&M deuren (ook achterwand uitvoeren als deuren)
dubbelzijdig gestoffeerd
te openen met drukknop-springsloten

Q&M corpus melamine rood

Q&M zijwanden gestoffeerd

Q&M rubber plint 30*15 mm 4mm terugliggend

aanzicht 1

Q&M opbergnis: achterwand + zijwanden vzv stoffering
AVEX voorzien AV-componenten + stalen afdekpaneel 626x106mm
v.z.v. rode coating RAL 3020
Q&M kabeldoorvoer voorzien

Q&M sleuf 20*600mm over ganse breedte van kast
tbv verluchting AV materiaal in kast

Q&M deuren dubbelzijdig gestoffeerd
te openen met drukknop-springsloten
Q&M corpus melamine rood
Q&M achterwand uitvoeren als 2 deuren,
dubbelzijdig gestoffeerd
te openen met drukknop-springsloten

GTI vanuit vloerdoos ø19mm naar plint kastje brengen tbv
AV-installatie, aantal aan te geven door GTI/AVEX

19" AV rack

Q&M rubber plint 30*15 mm 4mm terugliggend

doorsnede 1

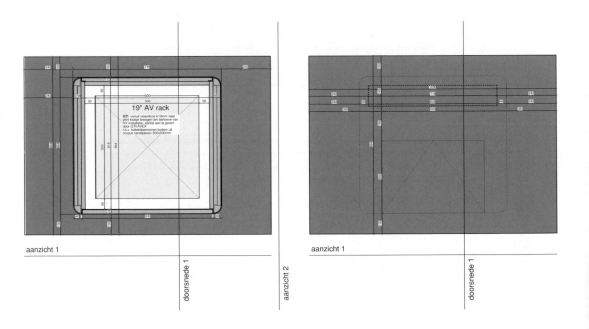

19" AV rack
GTI vanuit vloerdoos ø19mm naar
plint kastje brengen ten behoeve van
AV-installatie, aantal aan te geven
door GTI/AVEX
t.b.v. kabeldoorvoeren bodem uit
corpus verwijderen 500x500mm

aanzicht 1

doorsnede 1

aanzicht 2

aanzicht 1

doorsnede 1

The Internet Bookmobile

The Internet Bookmobile is a mobile digital library capable of downloading public domain books from the Internet via satellite and printing them anytime, anywhere, for anyone. Just like traditional bookmobiles that brought books to people in rural areas all over the world, the Internet Bookmobile will bring an entire digital library to a new generation of readers. Founded by Brewster Kahle, the Internet Bookmobile's goal is to provide universal access to all human knowledge. Part of accomplishing that goal is to make sure that public domain books are available digitally. Another part is making sure people across the country have access to those works whether by reading on screen, or more likely, to be printed back out again as a book. There are presently two Internet Bookmobiles in the United States, two in Egypt, one in Uganda and two in India with 28 more presently in the works for India.

Internet Archive
www.archive.org/texts/bookmobile
(last accessed 6 January 2005)

Camels as Bookmobiles

The Kenya national library system was founded in 1965 and has grown to consist of 23 library branches, eight bookmobiles, and two camel mobile units. The camel mobile units are used to bring library services to regions of Kenya not accessible by motorized transport. In each unit three camels are used to transport 300 books, a tent, and floor mats for setting up a temporary library branch.

Kenia National Library Service
www.knls.or.ke/camel
(last accessed 15 January 2005)

TO IMITATE KAGANOF'S STYLE. IF I DID I WOULD HAVE MISSED THE POINT...

...ANOF IS THAT YOU HAVE TO WRITE ABOUT LANGUAGE IN GENERAL...

...UAGE. YOU CANNOT IMITATE SOMEONE WHO DOES NOT IMITATE SOMEONE WHO...

DISCOURSE IN ORDER TO WRITE ABOUT DISCOURSE. MOREOVER, AS KAGANOF SUGGESTS...

FOR GOD ALONE. THIS IS WHY KAGANOF IS DIFFICULT TO READ BECAUSE HE DOESN'T...

...T GENEROUS ACT. SELFISH AND GENEROUS. WHEN KAGANOF READS...

...E DIFFERANCE IS THAT KAGANOF NEVER STOPS TALKING HE KEEPS ON WRITING...

...STAKE HERE IS A DECISION ABOUT THE FRAME...

...) IN RELATION TO THE WORK? ON THE EDGE? OVER THE EDGE?...

...T OF A PROJECTION OF THE MIND. PHILOSOPHY ALONE CAN POSE THE QUESTION...

...THE WORK OF ART. THE ORIGIN OF THE WORK OF ART IS THE ARTIST...

OPER OF THE ERGON, BUT ALSO FROM THE OUTSIDE, FROM THE...

...IT MERGES INTO THE WALL, AND THEN GRADUALLY INTO THE GENERAL TEXT...

WHERE DOES THE FRAME TAKE PLACE? DOES IT TAKE PLACE?...

...THIS IS A FUNDAMENTAL PRESUPPOSITION, PRESUPPOSING...

...METAPHYSICS, ONTO-THEOLOGY ITSELF...

...MUST BE IGNORANT TO HAVE A RELATION WITH BEAUTY BUT IN THE PRODUCTION OF BEAUTY...

NOWLEDGE WITH REGARD TO THE END DOES NOT INTERVENE AT THE END...

Facts on Paper

> a 50% increase in worldwide paper consumption is expected by 2010
> 115 billion sheets of paper are used annually for personal computers
> 700 pounds of paper are consumed by the average American each year
> 10,000 trees are cut down annually in China to make holiday cards
> 3 cubic yards of landfill space can be saved by one ton of recycled paper
> 77% of paper is recycled in the Netherlands
> 67% of paper is recycled in Germany
> 52% of paper is recycled in Japan
> 45% of paper is recycled in the United States

Sevin, J. (2000) Paper Chase
www.grist.org/news/counter/2000/02/02/paper
(last accessed 10 March 2005)

Sale of Books

The sale of books (excluding textbooks) in the Netherlands rose by 6.4% in 2004.
In 2002 the increase was only 0.4% and in 2003 there was rise of 4.9%.

NRC Handelsblad
www.nrc.nl /evj/artikel/1115874464843.html

No end to Paperwork

Not much more than a decade ago, we heralded computers, e-mail, and the Internet as a means to reduce
the consumption of paper for printing and writing, newsprint, packaging, and other uses. But today, more than ever,
computers and information technology have led to more paper consumption, not less. Far from ushering in a
"paperless" office, for example, computers, e-commerce, fax machines, and other information technologies have
fueled paper demand, creating more information consumers who routinely print web pages, e-mails, and other
verification of electronic information.

World Resources Institute, Earth Trends, The Environmental Information Portal
www.earthtrends.wri.org/index.cfm - (last accessed 15 January 2005)
Faostat Statistical Databases http://apps.fao.org/faostat/
(last accessed 17 May 2005)

Production of printing and writing paper
metric tons of paper
x 1000

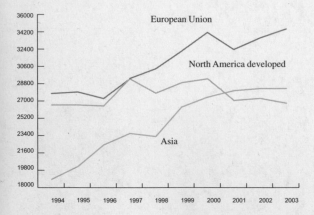

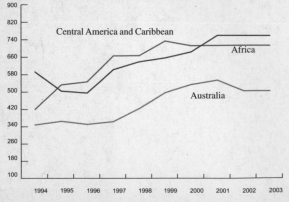

Previous page:
Aryan Kaganof, Sanctuary, Muti Galery
Johannesburg, South Africa, 2004

Librarians in Career Romance Novels

Career romance novels appeared in the US during the 1940s–1960s as women entered the workforce in increasing numbers. Publishers sought to exploit this demographic trend with books featuring accomplished and attractive young women simultaneously persuing their professional and romantic goals. Most of the books were written by professionals in their field, here by librarian authors starring heroine librarians who find love amidst the glamour of card catalogues, microfilm readers and bookmobiles.

www.jenw.org/home.htm
(last accessed 25 March 2005)

The Image of Librarians in Pornography

The librarian is a popular character in hardcore pornographic paperback novels. The librarian, most always portrayed as female, is depicted in a variety of types of libraries; public, academic, high school, special branches, etc. Often the library descriptions and situations make it appear as though the authors are either themselves librarians or frequent library users while others seem to have never even been in a library.
Below is a partial survey of a decade's worth of hardcore pornographic novels involving librarians published in the United States.

A Librarian's Training; A Librarian Enslaved; Bang the Librarian Hard; Eager Beaver Librarian; Helpful Head Librarian; Horny Hot Librarian; Horny Balling Librarian; Horny Peeping Librarian; Hot Bed Librarian; Hot Loving librarian; Hot Pants Librarian; Hot to Trot Librarian; Hot Mouth Librarian; In Heat Librarian; Lash the Librarian!; Librarian in Bondage; Librarian in Chains; Licking the Librarian; Line Up for the Librarian; Naughty Voyeur Librarian; Nympho Librarian; Overeager Librarian; Sally - Sexy Librarian; Sex Behind the Stacks; The Hottest Librarian; The Librarian Gets Hot; The Librarian Got Hot; The Librarian's Hot Fun; The Librarian's Hot Urges; The Librarian Loves It; The Librarian Slave; The Librarian With the Hots; The Oral Librarian; What a Librarian!

Previous page:
Copulation of clichés

Wings of Desire

Wim Wenders: The library [National Library in Berlin] was one of my favorite places but we didn't even have a permit to shoot there. No one had ever been allowed to shoot inside; there were always readers in there because they were never closed. Finally with some help from the mayor's side, they did allow us to shoot there. I don't know if you remember but we spent several Sundays in that library when there were no readers there.

Peter Falk: Everybody remembers that scene. I'll never forget it either. So many people I talked to remember the library. It had some kind of mood to it that you very rarely see. It was beautiful.

Wim Wenders: It comes also from the architecture itself. It's a really fabulous place done by somebody who really loves books. I mean most libraries you go to here you get a book and get the hell out of there. But this is the one place you really feel like sitting down and reading. You really feel protected. It's like a room made for….

Peter Falk: It's really wonderful….

Wim Wenders: Yes, yes you really feel that. The serenity in that building was tangible. One of the ideas of these voices was to treat them like music, especially here in the library that in my imagination was the place where the angels felt at home and where they lived.

Himmel über Berlin/Wings of Desire, directed by Wim Wenders (1987).
DVD release, A Road Movies Production, Berlin/Argos Film, Paris
Edited exerpt of Audio commentary by director Wim Wenders and
actor Peter Falk.

The UBU in 20 years time

BS: The library's central location makes it a suitable place of work for students and staff. I know for sure that the UBU will be a well-used building for the coming 20 years, with reading rooms, hundreds of places to study and books on open shelves. And I dare to predict that in ten years time our new library in De Uithof is the only library left; the small faculty libraries now in existence will not need a separate location anymore.

If the attraction of the collections is lost in the long term then this should be replaced by something else; this could be the function as a meeting-place. The library is already very important as a meeting-place now and this will become even stronger.

WA: The building is designed in such a way that if at a certain moment there are no more books in it, it could accommodate other programmes. The original idea was to give each of the faculties in the library their own, somewhat enclosed study area, each with its own style. That idea was dropped in the end. If we had done that it would have been much more difficult to make alterations. We have a much more neutral solution now, which means that Bas is very free in his programming; he can even bring in additional faculty libraries.

BS:The programme has changed considerably over the course of time. The hall in particular has altered, the journals room has disappeared and there are many more 'lounge' areas. If we were to start again I would make many more areas for group work. Changes in the educational programme mean that there is more and more demand for this.

WA: If I was starting on the design of the UBU now the building would contain another prgram for students, perhaps even with a swimming pool. Working on the new building may have given Bas more insight into how he would like the library to function in the future.

BS: The policy of the UBU is to integrate teaching and research as far as possible. This means that the library – as a function – is in fact less visible. The building, on the other hand, is very visible and as such is a symbol for the library in all its aspects.

Based on conversations with Wiel Arets, architect of the Utrecht University Library's new building and Bas Savenije, Director of the Library, held in 2004.

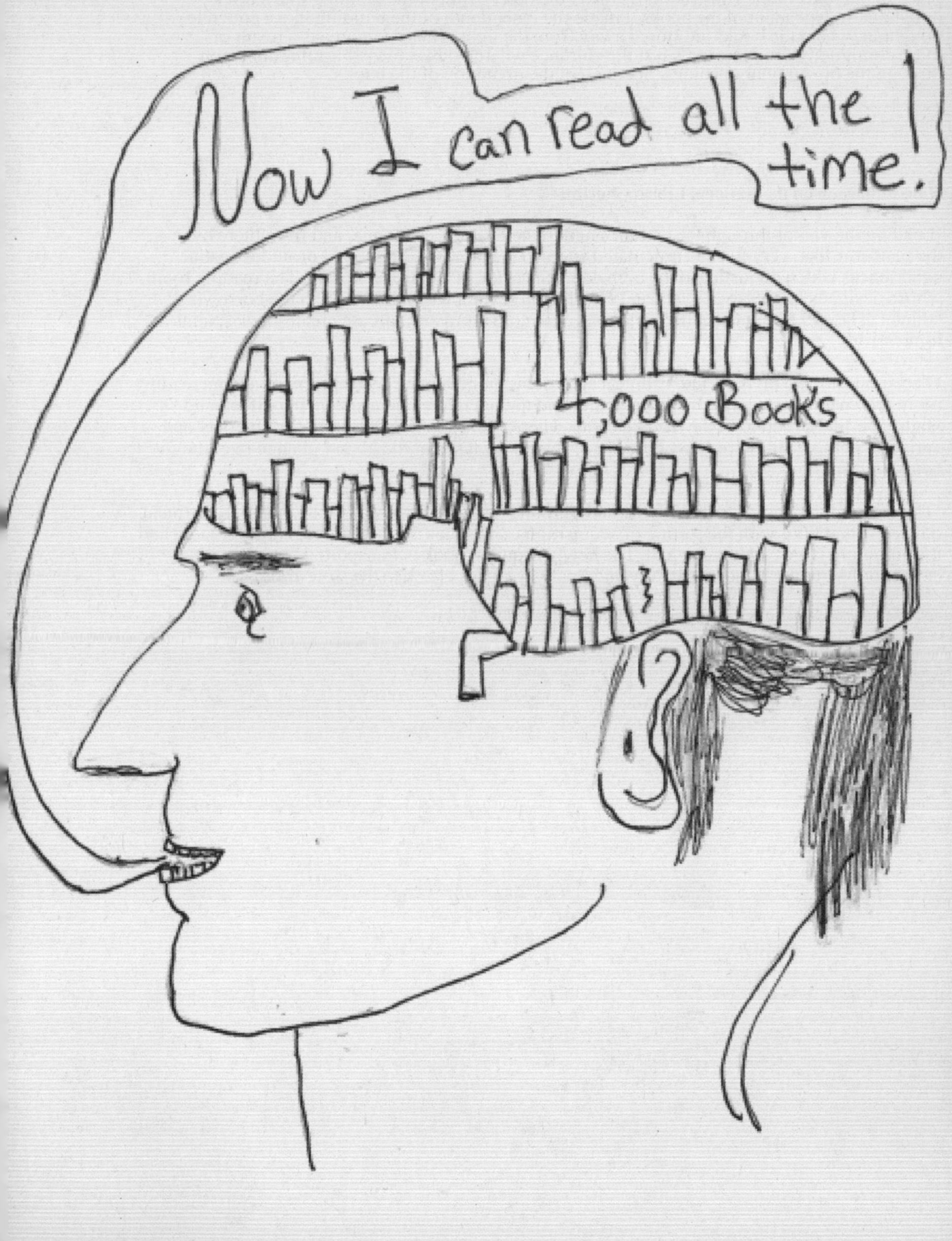
Now I can read all the time!
4,000 Books

According to Louis Kahn in 1965:

'Exeter began with the periphery, where light is. I felt the reading room would be where a person is alone near a window, and I felt that would be a private carrel, a kind of discovered place in the folds of the construction. I made the outer depth of the building like a brick doughnut, independent of the books. I made the inner depth of the building like a concrete doughnut, where the books are stored away from the light. The center area is a result of these contiguous doughnuts; it's just the entrance where books are visible all around you through the big circular openings. So you feel the invitation of the books'.

Louis Kahn about Library and Dining Hall, Phillips Exeter Academy,
Exeter, New Hampshire, us, 1965-1972
Source:David B. Brownlee, David G. De Long, Kahn, Los Angeles 1992

Hans Scharoun on the National Library Berlin:

'Leading the visitor through the entrance hall to the visitor's catalogue, and from there over the platform-like, very flat and articulated stairs to the large reading room, provides spatial experiences which do justice to the high demands made of a national library. The reading room, whose design is impressive, lively and effective in several ways links well to the borrowing counter. The exit through a gallery and a second more intimate staircase creates new spatial impressions'.

'The aim is not the division into cabinets and rooms, nor even the central form of a large reading room crowned with a dome, but the equality and mutual interchange enhancing effect, and landscape-like structure of the reading room. There is sufficient opportunity for diversity and variation in this 150-metre-long, fluid space should the tasks of the library change over the course of time'.

'The "way of the book" starts with the underground delivery; proceeds to the postal department on the ground floor with the sorting of acquisitions, continues through the registration room and the adjoining large cataloguing hall. The newly acquired book is transported from here on a conveyor belt to the in-house bindery and finally for a last check to the store-rooms'.

From Hans Scharoun's text with his entry for the 'Staatsbibliothek' competition, Berlin 30-5-1964
Hans Scharoun, Bauten, Entwürfe, Texte, herausgegeben von Peter Pfankuch, Berlin 1974, pp.339-355

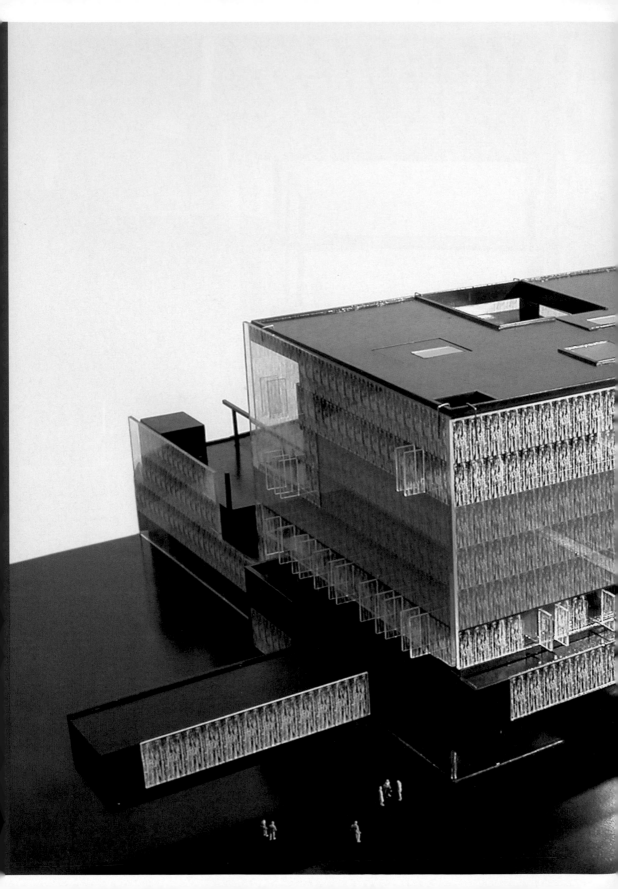

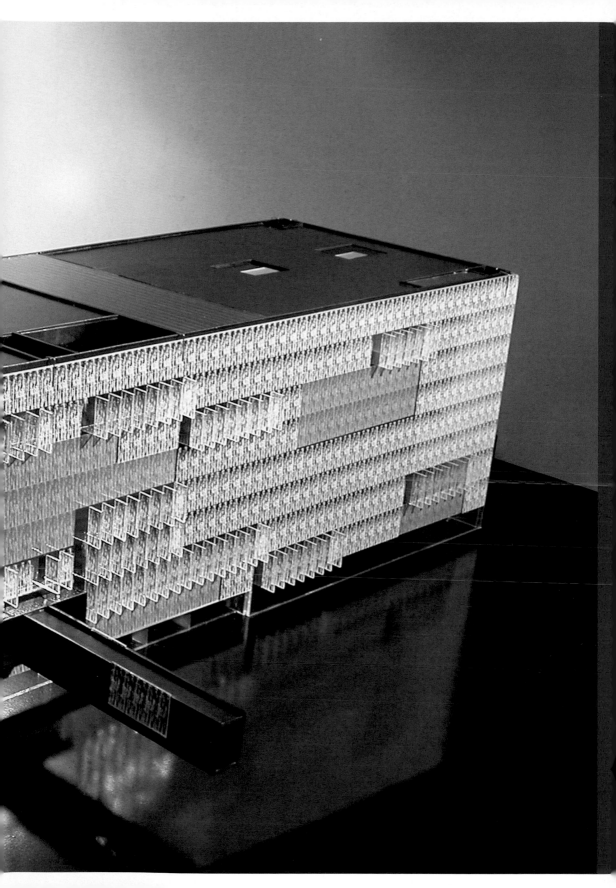

The Founding of the Utrecht University Library

The foundations for the present Utrecht University Library were laid in 1581. In that year the city fathers of Utrecht decreed that the books found in the Catholic chapters and monasteries could be seized as the city of Utrecht had been converted to Protestantism. With the books confiscated in this manner a city library was to be founded, which would be open to all. It was not until 1584 that enough books had been collected for a library to be actually set up. The collection consisted of 550-600 volumes, a not inconsiderable collection by the standards of the time. The canons of St. John's chapterhouse offered the choir of their church as a space for the library in the expectation that this would mean they would at least be assured of a 'worthy' use of their building. The library led a slumbering existence for years until around 1600 when it was offered two large legacies, from Huybert van Buchell, a former canon of St. Marie (around 2000 volumes), and from the legal scholar Evert van de Poll (around 1000 volumes). Together these collections laid the foundation for the Utrecht University Library. The city library was transformed from a theological book depot into a broadly oriented, up-to-date academic collection, for which a printed catalogue was even compiled. This was the first to be printed not in Latin but in the national language.

After the Illustre School was founded in Utrecht in 1634 (and later in 1636 turned into a university) the city library started to function as university library. The library gained an academic function and this meant a sharp increase in the number of visitors. The library gained its first librarian in the person of Cornelis Booth. He instituted regulations and embarked on a deliberate acquisitions policy. The Utrecht University Libraryi – still in its infancy – had come into existence.

The move to the former palace of Lodewijk Napoleon in 1820 brought a new flourishing period to the university. In the 20th century the library acquired a number of important collections as possessions or loans: the Central Old-Catholic library, the library of the Dutch Reformed church, the library of the Homeopathic Society and Simon Vestdijk's library. Additions are also currently being made to the collections of manuscripts and old prints. The additions are primarily concerned with Utrecht University, or the city or province of Utrecht. The collection of manuscripts has now grown to around 2850 manuscripts, at least 100,000 letters and some 2000 sets of lecture notes. The collection of old prints consists of around 100,000 works from before 1801 and a far greater number of works printed in the 19th century.

Vier eeuwen Universiteitsbibliotheek Utrecht, Utrecht 1986

Inventory UBU

584	600 volumes
1608	6000 volumes
1670	6175 books and 459 manuscripts
1718	ca. 7200 books and 479 manuscripts
1810	8699 books and 681 manuscripts
1855	26,592 titles (including journals)
1878	48,661 titles (104,253 volumes)
1939	250,000 titles (732,675 volumes)
1984	725,000 titles (3,750,000 volumes)
2005	2,090,000 titles (4,200,000 volumes)

Opening hours UBU

1640	Three afternoons in the week, professors also by appointment
ca. 1708	Wednesday and Saturday afternoon
ca. 1790	Several hours a week
1817	Monday and Thursday 13.00 – 15.00
	Tuesday and Friday 13.00 – 14.00
	Wednesday and Saturday 13.00 – 16.00
1849	Daily from 12.00 – 16.00 except Sundays
1913	Workdays from 10.00 – 17.00 and most evenings from 19.00 – 21.00
	In the academic holidays from 13.00 - 17.00
1970	Monday to Friday from 9.30 – 17.15 and from 19.00 – 21.45
2005	Weekdays from 9.00 – 22.30
	Saturday from 9.00 – 18.00
	Sunday from 12.00 – 18.00

Vier eeuwen Universiteitsbibliotheek Utrecht, deel I, Utrecht 1986
De Utrechtsche Universiteitsbibliotheek, Utrecht, 1909
Annual Reports Universiteitsbibliotheek Utrecht

Previous page:
Trinity College Library, Dublin

Wiel Arets interviews Toyo Ito
about the Sendai Mediatheque, Japan (2005)

1. What was your ambition in regard to the Sendai Mediatheque? I wanted to deviate, even if only slightly, from the hackneyed and boring public building of the Japanese management principle.

2. How could we read the programmatic condition of the project within the Japanese city and system? The idea of 'function' did not exist in the traditional architecture of Japan. It was integrated into another system – order - which was established only by a difference of place, like Ichi-no-ma (first room), Ni-no-ma (second room), Oku-no-ma (back room), Do-ma (earth floor). 'Sendai Mediatheque' aims to be architecture which is distinguished only by difference of 'place'.

3. The competition brief was to design a building combining different programs like an art gallery, public library, film & media centre and information centre. However, you changed that brief. Could you explain why? If there is anything to add to what I said under 2, you might say that this architecture artificially reproduces the space of nature like a forest. Activity in each place can be provisional and also be interchanged.

4. When you showed me the building I was surprised at the fact that each façade is designed differently. They look like they are as thin as a sheet of rice-paper sometimes transparent and some times translucent. Could you describe your design strategy concerning this glass façade in relation to the program and city context? Originally, the space was to be infinitely consecutive like a forest. The facade resembles a cutting plane like space being confined on the site: architecture in the realistic condition. The world (or universe) in which "conclusion" was shown whenever it was enclosed by the same façade, in spite of the covered transparent tube. Therefore, I wanted to avoid that.

5. The randomly penetrating circles create voids as if the vertical matter is rotten and only the irregular bone-like parts are remaining. Could you agree with this interpretation? For me, 'tube' holds a stronger image. The partition is not easily held up by organic-shaped and randomly arranged 'tubes' with different sizes. It means that I tried to make a space which was not at all like a homogeneous office. Moreover, the idea was to make it differ from a mere pillar by being a 'tube' in mid-air and it was able to strongly integrate the entire whole.

6. The structure, you worked on with Mutsuro Sasaki, is dominant and unique since it might neglect the supporting aspect. How would you describe this solution? After the 1990s, my expression went back and forth between transparent-cubic (e.g. Hotel-P, T-building in Nakameguro, etc) and fluid-organic (e.g. Shimosuwa Municipal Museum, etc). In the 'Sendai Mediatheque' I tried to unite those expressions by sealing the organic shaped 'tube' into the transparent 'tube'. Therefore, 'Sendai Mediatheque' became the beginning of the experiment related to various structures and space.

7. The building under construction looked like the development of a big machine, made out of steel parts to minimize the thickness of each part. Could this be described as a conscious concept? At first I thought of disappearing iron but later of it becoming a tube of light. When the overwhelming appearance of iron being welded in the construction site came to my eyes, I changed my concept. I wanted it to be stronger architecture by making the iron demonstrative.

8. What is your idea behind using different colours at night for each floor? By artificial light the skin of the building seems to disappear.
9. The furniture is designed by different architects and designers. Why?
In my first sketch this is described as "making floor height random". With this image, I intended to convey that each floor should have a different finish, different furniture and different lighting. It is because I wanted to show that the building had an existence independent of each floor.

10. What do you think about the position of the traditional book in the near future when we consider new media as a seemingly dominating source of information? The more the image media advance, the more the meaning of "Book" as "Material" grows. In the same way: the more the human brain evolves, the more man's body in contrast has meaning.

Wiel Arets interviews Dominique Perrault
about the Bibliothèque Nationale de France, Paris, France (2005)

1. You once said that the Bibliothèque Nationale de France is 'a place and not a building'. Could you elaborate on this statement? I said 'it is a landscape, it's not a building'. In this landscape you can find a special space, a huge void in the city between the four towers at each corner. This project's most important characteristic is the void, the empty space. Most of the building is underground, and only 25% is above ground around a garden, a piece of forest. All the rest is underground.

2. What was your personal interest in designing this intriguing building, which was the prize-winning entry to the competition for the Bibliothèque Nationale de France? This building is a monster. Its volume is huge: 300,000 m². The Centre Pompidou in Paris fits more than three times into it. The idea was to try and find a solution for the presence of this monster in the city, working with the paradoxical concept of the presence and absence of its architecture. Compared to the other 19 entries in the competition, this project is the lightest. The presence of nature in the centre contributes to that.

3. It seems that you are fortunate to produce mainly 'Grands Projets' like the French National Library in Paris, the Olympic Vélodrome and Swimming Pool in Berlin and the European Court of Justice in Luxembourg. Are these buildings a dominant factor within the development of the contemporary city? Yes they are a dominant factor. These kinds of cultural, sports or judicial buildings are very prominent in the city. The goal for me with these projects is to find out how to manage and control the presence of public space within these projects. Usually they are built with a big wall around; it is impossible to go through them. The Library is a huge institution but it gives permission to pass through. It is the same in Berlin and Luxembourg.

4. The four symbolic towers with wooden panels to control the climate expose the collection as a treasure to the public. But they also create an emptiness, which is often found in your work. Could you elaborate on the use of the wooden panels? For the offices in the basement of the tower, each wooden panel is movable. The levels above the offices in the basement are for storage, each with fixed wooden panels. The panels close the inside and a layer of glass is wrapped around it. The initial idea for the competition was to build the complete volume of each tower in glass. The finishing of the wooden panels would follow the growth of the collection step by step. Each year we would build one or more floors of the wooden panelling. But François Mitterand said: 'I have the money now, so all should be built now. After me there might be no money for the library anymore'.

5. 'A sea of trees, a froth of leaves' is how you describe the sunken garden. In nearly all your work the relationship with nature seems to be inevitable. Can you say more about your seeming obsession with nature? One idea is about transforming a building into a landscape. The other idea is to consider nature as material, just like concrete, metal or glass. The library's garden is really material; creating it was a building process. This kind of ambiguity is exciting: is it natural or artificial? For the visitors, the garden seems to be totally natural. A lot of people said to me that it was a very good idea to have kept the garden in the centre of the library and to build the building around it. They think that this garden existed before the library was built.

6. In all your work glass seems to be the favourite material for developing façades, which could be seen as filters. Where does this interest in what one could describe as osmosis come from? For me the façade should be a filter. With a glass façade all of the façade can be transparent or opaque, there's a choice. The light can be controlled; with curtains, coloured or (screen)- printed glass. Later inside and outside of the building can be combined; into the glass, or in between the glass. A special design can be developed with different materials to build a complex façade. This façade becomes like a filter, very efficient, special and sensitive.

7. The use of seemingly sterile materials like glass and woven steel in combination with wood seems to be a constant factor which gives your work a generous expression; how would you explain this warm atmosphere? There is no explanation; it's just me, it's my feeling. Architecture is a very heavy art, the physical presence of a building is never light. Working with materials like wood allows us to introduce a more sensual, sensitive and smooth feeling, which in the end gives more comfort.

8. When we visited the library, you used the word violence and you spoke about the forbidden as being an important word to explain your work. For me architecture is a violent action. To build a wall is a very strong decision; the wall will separate a space in two. Such a decision is an act of physical violence, to create a forbidden situation between one part and another. So for an architect it is very important to develop a specific attitude towards the quality and the status of the wall. And especially towards the materials to be used.

9. How would you describe research within your work and what is your interest within the academic field? The idea for me is to go beyond the academic field and merge other fields of knowledge – political, economic, ecological knowledge. My theory is: everything is material for architecture. I could manipulate all things to create a project; there is no limit. Material is something you work with, so a client – with his context – is material also.

10. Do we need books in the future and is a library within our contemporary society in which new media are dominant still a relevant topic? We are now working on the Digital Library of Korea, which will be an extension of the National Library in Seoul. It will be on the same site, connected to the existing building. But the new library is only for digital support, built into the hill on which the existing one was built. A library is absolutely a relevant topic for the future.

Wiel Arets interviews Jacques Herzog (Herzog & de Meuron)
about the Eberswalde Technical School, Germany (2005)

1. What was your personal interest designing this intriguing building, which is an extension to the existing Eberswalde University Library? Budget restrictions and lack of influence on internal organisation and therefore on the spatial innovation of the library were a serious problem in that project. The fascination of working in this remote city in the former DDR, however, was strong enough to seduce us.

2. Since this building is designed in collaboration with your friend Thomas Ruff, for whom you designed his house and studio in Düsseldorf, I have to ask you why Herzog & de Meuron (HdM) has this particular interest in collaborating with artists? As we know that you also decided to work with Gerard Richter if your design for the Jussieu Library would have been built. Our idea of using images in such an extensive way required the collaboration of a person professionally dealing with images. Such persons are artists rather than architects. Plus we knew that Thomas was collecting newspaper photos as a kind of personal historic archive. We were very keen to get access to this archive of images. Gerhard Richter's work has intrigued us for similar reasons – particularly his interest in the relationship of the natural and the artificial seems not far away from ours. Currently he has produced a huge mural for the main court of our New de Young Museum, opening in October 2005 in San Francisco's Golden Gate Park.

3. A pictorial historical narrative, in fact a classical theme within Swiss architecture, was the starting point for the façade. It is not the first time you worked according to this idea, why are you so interested in the façade and this addition of images onto the façade? Which Swiss tradition are you talking about? Images and ornaments have not been used in modern or contemporary architecture for decades, neither in Switzerland nor elsewhere. They were banned by Adolf Loos and other mainly protestant believers (namely also in Switzerland!). Façades are as important as all the other ingredients to create and produce architecture, such as space, form, programme. We use them all – sometimes giving more weight to one thing for reasons we cannot always dictate ourselves.

4. Is a library within our contemporary society in which new media are dominant still a relevant topic or do we have rewrite this typological construct? We don't have to rewrite or reinvent the library as a typology. We have to reinvigorate libraries because they remain fantastic places to read, to study, to meet, to hang around with books and people.

5. What will be the position of the book in the future? People will continue to read and smell them.

6. How would you describe research within the work of HdM, since it seems to be strongly related to the making? Research in all fields of architecture is at the basis of all we have ever done. Everything is research and experiment.

7. The court seems to be a continuous element in your work, whether we talk about the Koechlin House, the Hypobank, the Institute for Hospital Pharmaceuticals or your design for the Jussieu library. Could you elaborate on this issue?
The court has been one of the smartest, long-living and practical typologies in architecture for thousands of years. Why should we not use it when it seems appropriate?

8. Concerning research I would be interested in your opinion about the development of the contemporary city. Which contemporary city? They are all more and more different and specific. Globalisation has increased economic pressure on cities just like on individuals in their professional careers. The outcome is a kind of accelerated process of aging revealing specific weaknesses as well as strengths.

9. Your academic work is culminating in your Basel Institute. Could you elaborate on the work produced in this laboratory and your specific interest in this matter? We are examining exactly these processes of transformation and trying to understand how cities are changing and how eventually to influence such a process of change.

10. Studying with Aldo Rossi was for Pierre de Meuron and yourself important, as you mentioned that his provocative 'architecture is architecture' is still relevant for you. Could you tell me how you would describe yourself as an academic person besides being an architect. As I said before we are more experimental than academic. We have established our Basel Institute outside the Eidgenössische Technische Hochschule in Zürich for this very reason: to protect it from academic bureaucracy, which is a killer for everything new. Our research with cities and architecture, however, is producing and feeding an academic army of critics, teachers and students who will study, comment and digest this production. This we cannot and also do not want to prevent. We see it also as a chance that we live in a time with no urbanistic or architectonic theory. Practising, researching, criticising and studying architecture ideally go hand in hand with as little as possible bureaucratic organisation.

Wiel Arets interviews Rem Koolhaas
about the Public Library, Seattle, USA (2005)

1. What were your aims when you started the design? We had the ambition to find out what role a 1000-year-old typology could play in today's world, the ambition to find out what a public building means in the age of the market economy; to find out how we could make a progressive building in the America of today, and how we could mobilise the character – radical/visionary/ technological and cautious – that is specific to Seattle.

2. The voyeuristic attitude expressed by the building, determined largely by the entirely glazed envelope and continuous circulation route, sets up a discordant relation with the context. Was this for you a reason to make a building whose most salient characteristic seems to be communication? I'll leave the choice of adjectives to you, but I can say thing things about the context. Seattle is remarkable because of its unique and romantic topography, but the urban and architectural substance of the city itself is utterly generic. We deliberately avoided focusing on the sur-rounding grey skyscrapers. Instead, each platform is positioned so that it engages with the lyrical particulars of the surroundings, such as the volcano, Mount Rainier, the harbour, and the light.

3. Is the concept of 'Library' even applicable to the building in Seattle, given that it could be better termed a medium for communication? We studied which elements of the library needed to be modernised and which needed to be maintained... You could call it a modernised library.

4. The building occupies an entire city block and is inserted into the city fabric in ostensibly "American" fashion. Which raises the question: what determined the form of the building? As I said, it's a hardcore programmatic diagram, influenced by a lyrical context.

5. Did the fact that Microsoft and Boeing are based in this coastal city have any effect on the project or its programmatic conditions? The effects of Microsoft and Boeing were:
> Seattle is one of the few places left in the world where the belief in rationalism is still intact.
> Openness for the issue of technology.
> General intelligence of participants in the whole process. The board included permanent representatives from Microsoft and Boeing, and there was both personal interest and generosity from Bill Gates and Paul Allen, Microsoft billionaires from the very beginning.

6. The structural facades of glass and steel look like they were formed as a single module and fold around the artificial interior landscape like a porous skin. Why the uniform facade treatment? The library is a municipal building, built with a municipal budget. The architecture could only meet expectations through the development of a system in which structure and cladding form one entity. Hence the module, which is both structural and optimised in terms of size of glazing and fabrication.

7. Gary Hill, the Seattle-based artist, made a video for the library. How do you view the role of art and the work of an artist inside a building you designed, in the knowledge that many architects currently involve artists in the process of producing design concepts? I think the 1% rule – the regulation that makes art mandatory – is a disaster. For both architect and artist. I think that cooperation of this sort mainly serves to shroud the identity crises afflicting both of them. I'd love to make architecture without art and I find it ridiculous I can't. Having said that, Tony Oursler is a friend, and with him I've tried to remove the "mandatory" by enabling him to destroy a piece of the building. In other words, we didn't dodge the violence that comes with combining Art and Architecture.

8. As far as I know, the collaboration with Maarten Van Severen dates back to the design of the house in Bordeaux. He was also involved in the theatre for Porto, a building that features carpets by Petra Blaisse. Can you tell me about your structural collaboration with such people? The collaboration with both Maarten Van Severen and Petra Blaisse dates back to the mid-1980s and is based on the simple knowledge that they are uniquely talented, and that it's better to avail of their talents rather than try and perfect them ourselves. I fundamentally like collaboration and have been able to follow the progression of both Van Severen and Blaisse from close by without being responsible for it in any way. I hate the class phobia that architecture often implies and have always been fascinated by the idea of giving individuals like these the space that I couldn't or wouldn't claim for myself.

9. Is this the ideal library? Or rather, how would you criticise it as a journalist? Just give it a go, I'd say. Know anyone still intent on pursuing ideals today?

10. What role remains for the book now and in the near future, given that we are surrounded by new media? Over the past 30 years I've witnessed the inexhaustible vitality of the book. And I find it fascinating to see how new technology influences the book. SMLXL is inconceivable without the whole notion of hypertext, but it's still essentially a book. I think that the relation between man and book has an intimacy unrivalled by other media.
So it's unlikely the book will ever disappear.

FLYING STONES
Project for the Library

The interior of the building is a Borgès labyrinth opening on several levels, a succession of perspectives on sequences of falsely aleatoric spaces, both private and communal. Too complex to grasp in a single image and defying a purely spatial description, it should be reconstructed in the form of a narrative, a story.

Its black colour is the emotional dimension of the space. It evokes a cave, an interior landscape, but open to the outside. The concrete blocks in which the archives are kept seem to be suspended in space. The building loses its mass. These concrete clouds recall the floating rocks that appear in certain paintings of Magritte.

The surface of the building – walls and panes – is covered by a copy-and-paste of a plant-like pattern in the Rosetta stone, the matrix of a Gutenberg book, or a screen. At the user's request, the books circulate within this organism as a result of an interior network.

The intention is to produce a virus, an intruder that moves around within this interior landscape. The movement of this object must be in accordance with the temporality that implies the act of reading. Something must stir slowly, must distract.

The effect must be that of a tortoise moving around in the garden. A shape moving in a natural landscape, an earthly landmark, an endemic shape. It could be part of the building, a unity, one of these patterns, which having separated is circulating in space.

A piece of concrete, a stone floating above the heads of readers and moving very slowly. This unity must be multiplied. A multitude of movements, five or six floating unities must be envisaged. Their entire movements will have to be choreographed.

Pierre Huyghe

Saint Catherine of Alexandria

Born to the nobility, Saint Catherine was educated in science and oratory. At the age of 18 she presented herself to the Roman Emperor Maximus to protest against his violent persecution of Christians. Astounded at her audacity in upbraiding him for his cruelt, but incompetent to vie with her in the matter of learning, he summoned numerous scholars in an attempt to defeat her in argument. Contrary to expectations, she managed to convert his scholars with her eloquence and her knowledge of religion and science. The Empress together with Porphyry, the leader of Maximus's army, were so amazed by Catherine's stories that they went to see her where she was being held prisoner. During their visit, they too were converted. An enraged Maximus ordered Catherine broken on the wheel, but when it touched her, the wheel burst into pieces. She was subsequently beheaded.

Her reputation for wisdom and learning led her to be named the patron saint of archivists and librarians. She is most often portrayed clutching her books by the wheel.

The Catholic Community Forum
www.catholic-forum.com/saints/saintc01.htm

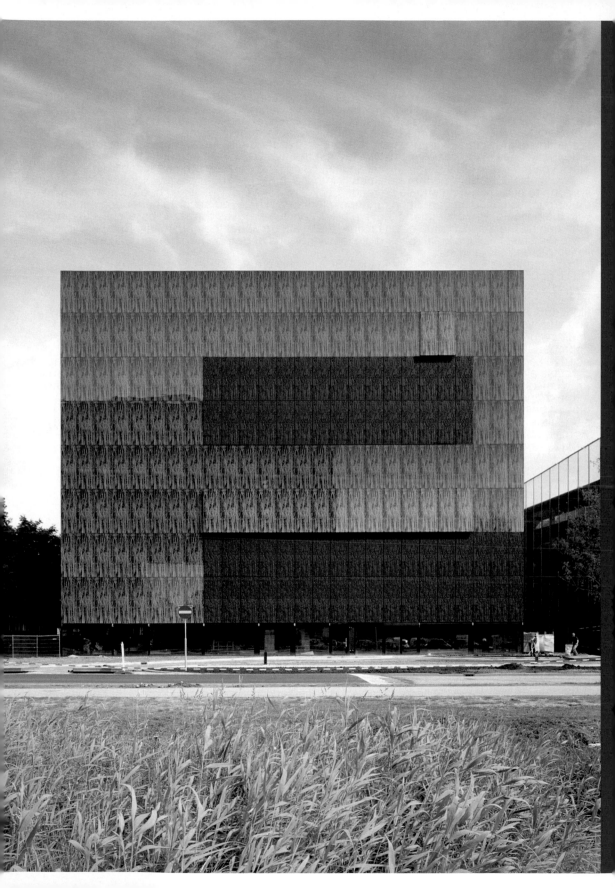

THE QUASI-OBJECT
Purity and Provocation in Wiel Arets's Utrecht University Library

From a distance the new library by Wiel Arets Architect and Associates on De Uithof campus looks impenetrable. A gigantic black rectangular box with grey windows snuggles mysteriously between De Uithof's countless different buildings. By revealing itself as a monochrome mass, it creates a sense of calm and order in the rather chaotic context of the campus. The purity and perfection of the volume surprises in the same way as the rectangular monolith that appears among the apes in the desert in the Stanley Kubrick film 2001: A Space Odyssey. The huge black volume of the UBU is impressive and imposing, and raises more questions than it answers. It is not a building that slots neatly into the thinking of user or viewer, nor does it conform to how a building should be read: "Look, I'm a library!" But, like a book, it is a machine that provokes one to embark upon further exploration. When you become better acquainted with the building, you understand that the black concrete houses the static book collection and that, behind the monochrome glass façade, the users go about their business. But there is more than just this functional reading of massive clouds of books interspersed with transparent reading areas.

In its manifestation and positioning the UBU not only creates order in the disorder of De Uithof, but also opens up different metaphorical readings of the black box. Many writers consider a library to be a prison where knowledge is locked safely away, and this is one way of understanding the black world of the volume in Utrecht. The library could also be seen as a flight data recorder where all the moves of civilisation are recorded – just like the black box in an aeroplane, bursting with information that enables us to reconstruct where errors occurred and how problems could have been circumvented. Yet another black box refers to the black chamber of a camera where the incoming light is transformed into a new image. We do not need to know how the transformation in the black box of the camera happened: the result, the output is all that matters. In the abstract engine room of the black box, decisions are taken and problems solved, unseen by the outside world. Somehow the black volume of the library refers to the divine, as described by Umberto Eco: "… a library is the best possible imitation, by human beings, of a divine mind, where the whole universe is viewed and understood at the same time. A person able to store in his or her mind the information provided by a great library would emulate in some way the mind of God. In other words, we have invented libraries because we know that we do not have divine powers, but we try to do our best to imitate them.[1]" Whether the black volume represents "divine power" or not, it challenges us all to constantly forge new relations.

The quasi-object

To better understand the world, modern science, over a period of roughly 200 years, has divided our hybrid reality into two cultures. On the one hand, human sciences explore the "soft" dimensions of our existence – which social categories are projected onto an object – while the natural sciences concentrate on the intrinsic, "hard" dimensions of the object. In the human sciences, the object has no meaning as a thing; it only exists to be used as a white screen onto which society projects its ideals. For the natural sciences, the objective powers of the thing are so strong that they alone are of overriding importance. It is this duality of objects between the "soft" and "hard" that must be urgently reconsidered when we attempt to evaluate the innovative quality of the UBU.

Traditional architectural criticism and history are concerned with form, the style in which an object is built. How the monochrome form of the UBU will colour the life of the community will always elude it. It is precisely as if, in most reflections on architecture, narratives of use are totally divorced from the diverse architectural qualities of an object. Time and again, it goes unnoticed that objects only acquire meaning once their cultural capital is activated by different formations of use in context and time. Things are imparted meaning by use and perception, by touch, by looking at and being looked at, by habit and tactile appropriation, by a coincidental discovery during a walk or conversation. As theoretician Marian Fraser observed, "Matter does not 'exist' in and of itself, outside or beyond discourse, but is rather repeatedly produced through performativity, which brings into being or enacts that which it names.[2]" The research into either the "hard" or "soft" qualities of an object is naturally applied in practice, but how these two cultures function together, forming a complex whole, goes unnoticed. This is remarkable to say the least because in reality we do not make a distinction between two cultures; quite the opposite, we assume hybrid relations. For this reason, the researchers Michel Serres and Bruno Latour propose that we should cast the "soft" or "hard" object from our minds.[3] It is better to talk of the quasi-object. The quasi-object equips us to develop a new model of knowledge that goes beyond dividing an object into two cultures. Rather than considering an object as a fact or a value, to see it simply as a (stylistic) form or social function, we must begin to grasp the facts/values as intrinsically interrelated wholes. The point of a quasi-object is that relationships are forged between values and facts by different frameworks. The skin of a building is then not just an outside, a sculpture that demands our attention like Frank Gehry's Bilbao museum, but a membrane where outside and inside meet and merge.

When we come nearer to the UBU we see that the outer skin of the building – whether concrete or glass – is tattooed with a texture based on a close-up photo of willows by photographer Kim Zwarts. Through the tattooing of the skin of the volume between which sunlight and outside vista are filtered simultaneously, the naked functional body of the library object, the seemingly "hard" dimension, acquires a "soft" dimension. When you get closer to the UBU the massive nature of the building volume suddenly changes into a giant willow forest behind which books and people can be deciphered. When the many glass panels of the skin automatically open – like a flower opening to the sun - we discover that the library is composed of various public domains with views over the landscape of the University of Utrecht.

Such a skin integrates all the milieus that play a role inside and outside, and consists, just like human skin, of a variety of mixed feelings. Through "the skin, the world and the body touch, defining their common border, contingency means mutual touching: world and body meet and caress in the skin," comments Serres.[4] Neither the projection on ... nor the objective fact are central in a quasi-object, but the relations and interferences which are activated by the framing at different scale levels. The whole is held together by that which agitates or constantly attempts to pull it apart and bring it back together. The quasi-object is an astonishing constructor of intersubjectivity. "We know, through it," says Serres, "how and when we are subjects and when and how we are no longer subjects." "We": what does that mean? We are precisely the fluctuating moving back and forth of "I". The "I" in the game is a token exchanged. And this passing, this network of passes, these vicariances of subjects, weave through the collection... The "we" is made by the bursts and occultations of the "I". The "we" is made by the passing of the "I".[5] A quasi-object then is about inserting itself between, to underline that we live only by relations.

A landscape of encounters

From the outside, the library appears to be a treasure chest full of jewels over which a skin stretched taut not only serves a visual function but offers protection and allows it to breathe. Books are safe there and are protected against too much light. When visitors enter the building – by a stately meandering stairway on the ground floor or footbridge on the first floor – the library opens in gradual stages. On the ground floor, visitors enter a modest space, see the café and terrace to the left of the entrance, feel at home and become curious about what awaits them. The monumental staircase takes the visitor to the very core of the building. On entering the building a ritual unfolds that strongly resembles coming across the secret code that opens an antique treasure chest. The floor is a gleaming grey-white 'carpet' – that increasingly widens – taking the visitor to the heart of the library. Once in the nucleus of information we are confronted with an enormous void. Suddenly the visitor discovers that this library is not massive at all, but open and transparent, that you move between the potent black clouds of concrete full of books. Contrary to most libraries where you are pushed aside by kilometres of books, this one is comprised of open spaces for people. In this library, there is an integrated concept of five reading rooms, 470 study places, offices, book depots, a café, and shops on the ground floor, an exhibition area annex auditorium and a reading room where visitors and staff meet in their quest for knowledge and information. Like the State Library by architect Hans Scharoun in Berlin, this library incorporates an inward-oriented public landscape of different platforms, voids, routes and stairways threaded together to form a colossal network of floor fields. If you follow your route through the library – in search of a book, a colleague or a new love – you discover that all the many paths lead to the large urban square in the monumental void. On your route you can enjoy the view over the library from different balconies. Or you might decide to work alone, or together, in one of the open or closed areas.

In our information age of digitisation, consumption and far-reaching individualisation, the importance of the public sphere is often underestimated. While people attempt to re-invent public space in all manner of ways, commerce annexes and controls what was originally free public space. Most design decisions today are determined by consumer behaviour and budget rather than freedoms of choice that carry weight in other areas. What the architect Wiel Arets and principal Bas Savenije in Utrecht have fully grasped is that, in our privatised society, it is more important than ever to focus on the classic function of the library as a public space. The library as public institution is ideally placed in society for offering other forms of freedom; investing in encounters that can flourish independently of profit alone. The essence of a library is more than simply documenting and providing access to information. A library is a social centre with a multiplicity of responsibilities. If you spend your day at the computer, eyes red from staring at the screen, meet no one, rely on a costly piece of equipment that makes it impossible to sit and read in comfort, love a book's fetishistic quality, delight in discovering fresh leads, yearn to finger print, adore collecting, enjoy leafing through bookcases, take pleasure in the fact that you don't need a manual to scan a book's contents, can zap more quickly through a book than any software programme, don't risk blowing up your computer by spilling coffee on a page, then you long for a "classic" library where people and books find each other. With the UBU our society is not only investing in an advanced distribution centre packed with digital information that flows to different private domains, but also making room for a rich public domain unsullied by commercial interests. Knowledge and human interaction are at the heart of a library, not shopping.

Provocative purity

In both the library of architect Wiel Arets and the library of Rem Koolhaas's OMA in Seattle the books and offices of the staff are housed in secure and robustly closed boxes that seem to float in an integrated environment of open fields and routes packed with public activities and reading areas. Rem Koolhaas throws a transparent net over his massive zigzag stack of clouds. The Koolhaas library resembles a kind of diamond. Wiel Arets conceals his black book-clouds in semi-transparent treasure chest. Both palaces of memory behave like quasi-objects; they astonish, question, and establish a dynamic presence with their unconventionality. All the same, the dissimilarities are pregnant. The pure minimalism of Arets is nothing like the "Pulp Fiction" of Rem Koolhaas. Koolhaas invites the public to take possession of the building with references to the surrealism of everyday life in the city. OMA's library has a striking resemblance to a stage set from the theatre and film world. With the insertion of pieces of décor, he directs how various scenarios are staged by the user. OMA's library is all about content and meaning. Conversely, Arets opts for the intensity of emptiness. It is not surrealism informed by a collage of semantic urban images or programmatic content which inspires Wiel Arets but the provocative purity of material and form, the way volume and structure are present in space. Koolhaas celebrates the paradigm of endless difference while Arets enjoys the luxury of sameness, that which remains constant over time.

Arets's library differs through its emphasis on emptiness, familiar from the photographs of artist and photographer Thomas Demand and the film Dogville by Lars von Trier, where white chalk-lines on black asphalt imply abstractly and in essence the delineations of the village. The photos of Demand are images of absence. His photographs of crime scenes show no trace of the individuals who once inhabited them. The action has vanished from the image. Demand's intriguing mysteries raise questions about events that are not themselves present in the work. They incite thought and borrow their power from the persistent uncertainties that emanate from the constellation of objects. Arets's library functions similarly to the installations Demand constructs and his photographs. It is an architecture which lacks human traces and augmentations. If you look closely, you will see that the installations of objects in Demand's photographs of everyday places are paper models. There is an absence of any detail that could reveal how the models have been constructed or used. The handrails of Arets's library have a similar lack of detail. Just how the handrail is affixed to the floor remains invisible. Walls, windows and doors seem to fit seamlessly together without the intermediary of complicated connections. Floors and ceilings have been treated as pure planes. Cameras, cables, lighting, air conditioning and other details that could disrupt the overall abstraction have been rendered invisible. It is all about the purity of material, the construction and the volume, the rawness of the black and grey, to provoke the mystery of life.

Just as in photography that requires us to find the point – what Roland Barthes calls the 'punctum' – which brings the story of the photo to life, the UBU only comes alive when taken possession of by books and people. The dynamism of history and life imbues the building with colour. The building itself is monochrome. All the horizontal fields are grey. The vertical planes are black. The ceiling is as raven as a dark, star-spangled sky. Above all, the building is itself. Its monochrome purity challenges users to make it their own. The building is not a completion of life, but an invitation to it. It is a building like a blackboard that waits, in rapt anticipation of life's traces. The building comes to life as colour finds its way into it, in the guise of books or individuals. That is why it is unwise to judge the university library and also other buildings by Arets as autonomous objects. It is only through their definition as quasi-objects that we can really know which stories can unfold in the library. Photos of the building without its use or surroundings – its life – in fact hide how well Arets's buildings anticipate their use and the urban life which organises and gives form to the building.[6] Precisely because the building itself is monochrome, the life of both the visitors as well as the history of the book receive ample space to show their colours. And just at the point where the visitor and the building come into contact with each other in public the information counters are a provocative lipstick red, just like the red-hot Rolling Stones lips. Throughout the building, the red counters are fashioned of soft scarlet leather, exceptionally human in their pure, vivid hue. It is the way in which the building as organisation and form actualises the perception of use that makes Arets's library so captivating.

Representing the collective

In both the library of Scharoun in Berlin and in the library of Koolhaas, the movement of the library's programme (content) inspires the form, the material and the construction. There is every reason for both architects to wrap the façade around the content. In contrast, Arets hides the concept of the meandering routes of Scharoun's library in an absolutely monumental box so that the richness of the individual routes and the openness of the library remain hidden from the city. Arets works with two different systems; on the one hand the programme as infrastructure and on the other hand relatively autonomous and classical architectural elements. Like architect Louis Kahn, Wiel Arets seems to draw a distinction between "served" and "servant space". The "servant space" houses service functions such as the staircases, lifts and air conditioning. In so doing, the "servant space" frees the "served space" for human activities. For Kahn, the "servant space" has a function other than to serve; it expresses the institutional dimensions of a building by its monumental ordering principle. In this way, the brick chimneys of the Kahn Richards Medical Research Building in Pennsylvania are reminiscent of the fortified towers of the Italian town of San Gimignano. The symbolic meaning that Kahn expresses with his "servant space" proceeds in neutral terrain. In other words, he is searching for sustainable, collective values that, regardless of actuality, are of eternal symbolic value. Through actualising Kahn's principles anew Arets seems to have found a path which turns away from that of various contemporary architects who allow themselves to be inspired by the paradigm of difference without taking heed of the principles which should apply to all. In our culture of sprawl every form of collective representation has been lost. We live in an endless chaos of lifestyle collages without any expression of the common good or collective orientation. It seems as if Arets with his monumental black box, his "served" and "servant" space, is looking for collective expressions which leave both room for the multitude (paradigm of difference) as well as trying to solve the issue of the crisis of collective representation. Arets seems to believe in the representative power of the quasi-object, by which a building, through the puzzling beauty and luxuriousness of its elements and architectural principles, can create order and offer space to the multitude. Somehow he prefers a fixed ground and pure form against which the dynamic and uncertain events of life can unfold.

Arets is fascinated by quasi-objects – not objects that refer to eternal or neutral values, but quasi-objects that challenge the viewer, expose the institution in all its strange and luxurious purity. The use of monochrome and the repetition of the rows of black bookcases refer to Kafkaesque situations that abound in every library. A library holds an infinite categorised past; behind every door is another door leading to yet another world. The search never ceases. The archive absorbs ever-more information and knowledge, never stops archiving. You can wander through a library forever, perpetually discovering new scents, new doors that open for you. In the introvert realm of the library you can travel endlessly past words and images that our culture has noted and archived. It is this complex world that, with his quasi-object in Utrecht, Arets articulates in all its purity and provocation.

Roemer van Toorn

Notes
1. Umberto Eco, "Vegetal and mineral memory: The future of books", Al-Ahram, weekly On-line, 20 - 26 November 2003 (Issue No. 665)
2. Marian Fraser, "Classing Queer: Politics in Competition", in *Performativity and Belonging*, Vikki Bell ed. Theory, Culture & society, 1999.
3. "Quasi-objects are much more social" says anthropologist and philosopher Bruno Latour, "much more fabricated, much more collective than the 'hard' parts of nature, but they are in no way the arbitrary receptacles of a full-fledged society. On the other hand they are much more real, nonhuman and objective than those shapeless screens on which society – for unknown reasons – needed to be 'projected'." Bruno Latour, *We Have Never Been Modern*, Harvard University Press, Cambridge, MA, 1993.
4. Michel Serres, *The Parasite*, Johns Hopkins University Press, 1982.
5. Michel Serres, *The Parasite*, Johns Hopkins University Press, 1982.
6. It is curious to note that the use (content) of OMA buildings seldom needs to be photographed. The buildings are from the start only content. Daily life in many cases is already completely incorporated into the material and structure of the OMA project. This brings us to the interesting question of the extent to which organisation and form should indeed incorporate everyday reality (the programme) or leave it free. Are Koolhaas's buildings not already complete before use takes possession of them because all forms of use are already predestined by the architect as director? And on the other hand why are Arets's buildings always photographed out of use while the relationship between the object and its use give the architecture its real quality?

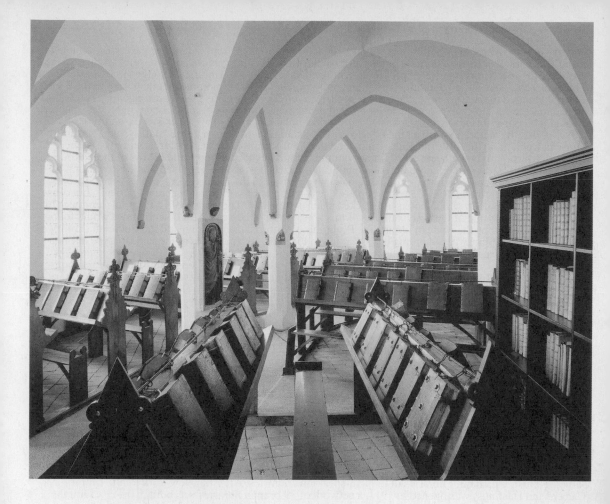

211

The Library through History

A library is both the room or building in which a collection of books is kept, as well as the collection itself. Not a single Greek or Roman library has survived, so the modern library as we know it stems from the Middle Ages. The first buildings that were specially constructed or furnished as libraries belonged to monasteries or universities and were situated mainly in England or France. The most famous academic library in the 13th century belonged to the Sorbonne, the college of the University of Paris. Its interior arrangement, with books chained to lecterns and each pair of lecterns situated near a window to catch sufficient daylight, was much imitated. Of course this arrangement wasted a great deal of space; an improvement was the addition of shelves above the lectern to form a kind of alcove. This arrangement known as the 'stall system' was used mainly in England in the 14th and 15th century and there are a number of such libraries still in existence. A later, but surprisingly well-preserved library built in the medieval tradition is the Librije of the Walburgs-kerk in Zutphen (1564). In all these libraries significant space is devoted to the reader. There is a striking change in the use of space in libraries of the Renaissance period. In the 'wall system' or the 'Saal-System' as it is appropriately termed in German, the emphasis lies on a spacious, impressive, empty perhaps, but often richly decorated room in which books are stacked against the walls. The library of El Escorial (architect Juan de Herrera, 1567) is one of the first examples of this type. Around the year 1600 other libraries would follow this example, including the Vatican library, the Bibliotheca Ambrosiana in Milan and the Bodleian Library in Oxford. The 'wall library' would remain popular in the 17th and 18th centuries as the standard type of library.

The interior of many libraries took the form of a Gesamtkunstwerk in which wall and ceiling paintings, wood-carving, reliefs, free-standing sculptures, bookcases and books form a single unified whole. Libraries like this are mainly found in southern Germany, Austria, Italy and Spain. Famous examples are the library of Melk Abbey (Jacob Prandtauer, 1730) and the Hofbibliothek in Vienna (Fischer von Erlach, 1726). In England a different course was pursued. With his library built for Trinity College in Cambridge in 1676, Sir Christopher Wren introduced a combination of the medieval stall system and the wall library. This was much more classical in design than the libraries in southern Europe. Longitudinal rooms with wall-shelving and sometimes galleries to use the space better were standard up to the middle of the 19th century. The Playfair Library Hall in the University of Edinburgh (William Playfair, 1827) is a renowned example of this style. As the number of books increased so did the height of the bookcases, and galleries or balconies had to be added. In the 19th century book ownership grew so much that walls alone could no longer provide sufficient space. This problem was solved by separating the reading space from the stacking area and the offices. This three-zone separation was to become the accepted organisation of library space for a long time to come. It was used for the two most important new libraries of the time, the Bibliothèque Nationale in Paris (Henri Labrouste, 1868) and the British Museum Library (Sydney Smirke, 1857). From now on, the main visual emphasis in libraries would be on the reading area. As in the medieval period the reader was paramount, but now surrounded by a selection of the library's books.

The golden age of library building dawned. Many national and municipal libraries were built, sometimes on the initiative of the authorities and sometimes financed by philanthropic organisations such as the Carnegie Trust, which built libraries in English-speaking countries. After the New York Public Library (Carrère and Hastings) was opened in 1911, a network of 39 branch libraries was built in the city with the assistance of steel magnate Andrew Carnegie. In other countries such as the Netherlands many libraries were built in the early 20th century as a result of the socialist fight for workers' emancipation. These library buildings, which were centrally situated and attractively designed, often acted as community centres as well. Scandinavia also contributed to making libraries both important and everyday places in the community. In the Stadsbiblioteket (1927) in Stockholm, Sweden, Asplund created an enormous circular reading room using the classical scheme of the centrally-planned library. In his version the readers are completely surrounded by a continuous wooden circle of books on all sides. For the Municipal Library in Viipuri (1935), Finland, Alvar Aalto separated connected spaces by differences in floor level. He surrounded these spaces by two levels of bookshelves. These Scandinavian libraries express the openness and democracy which would be demanded by modern society in the decades to come.

The Centre Pompidou in Paris (Rogers and Piano, 1976) has become the international example for a new generation of libraries: approachable, flexible and multifunctional. This Parisian library and its imitators function in fact as 'cultural department stores'; in making use of new technologies they are designed for mass consumption. This trend is continued in recent – mainly public – libraries which emphasise their desire to belong to the 'information society'. University libraries now have a double role: not only are they places for students to work and meet but they also play a major part in the access to and production of information. The Utrecht University Library (Wiel Arets, 2004) is a good example of this. Large, prestigious public libraries often take the shape of 'media-polis' which also act as a generator and catalyst for major urban regeneration schemes. Their remarkable appearance contributes to their role as a status symbols in every city that aims to be a hub within the international information network. According to Rem Koolhaas there is a danger that innovation is limited to the packaging. He sees a future only for the library that 'transforms itself wholeheartedly to aggressively orchestrate the coexistence of all available technologies to collect, condense, distribute, read and manipulate information'. Rather than being a space to read, the library is transformed into 'a social centre with multiple responsibilities'. Koolhaas's Seattle Public Library (2004) expresses this concept in built form.

Brawne, M., Bibliotheken, Libraries, Teufen 1970
Brawne, M., Library Builders, London, 1997
N. Pevsner, A history of building types, Washington 1976
Exhibition Bibliopolis, the library and the city 1850-1990, NAi, Rotterdam, Dec. 2004 - April 2005
www.oma.nl/oma.htm (last accessed 26 January 2005)

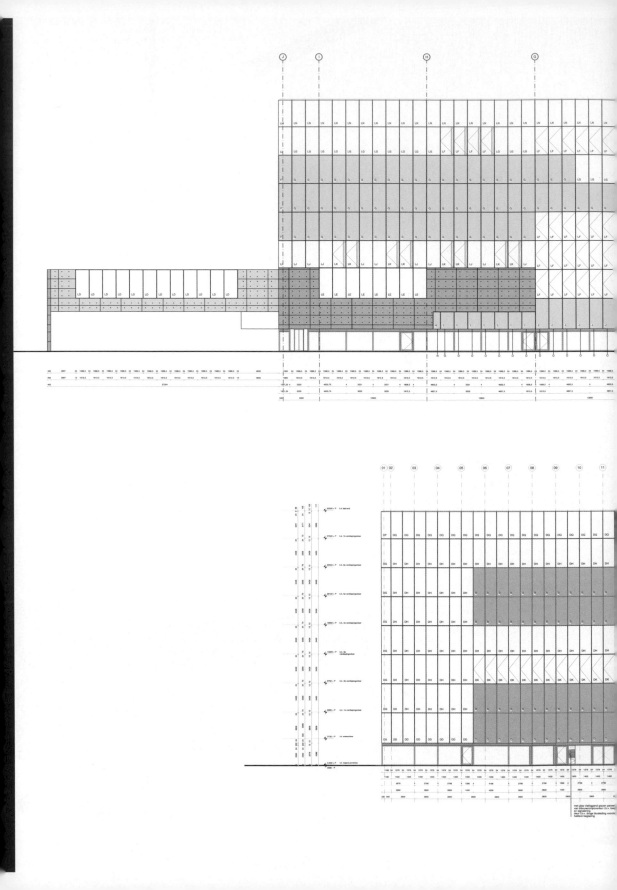

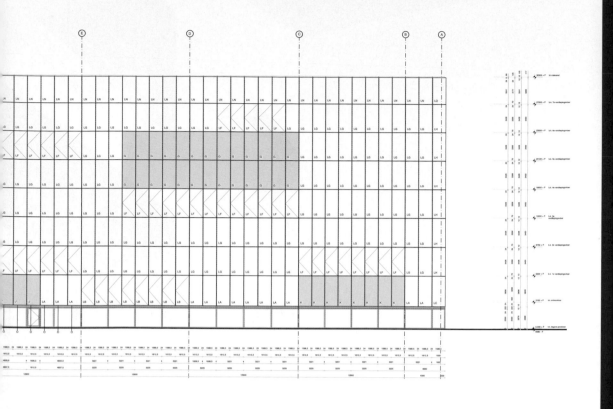

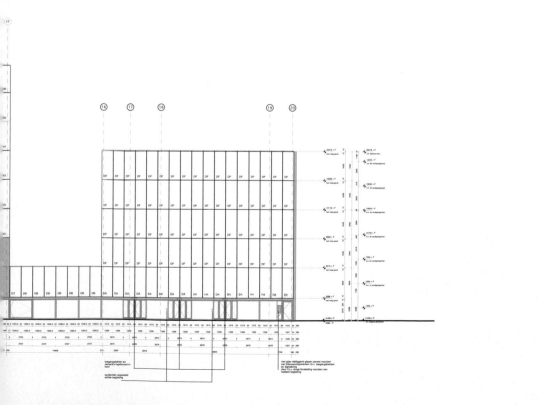

detail D.V.G.016   detail D.V.G.019

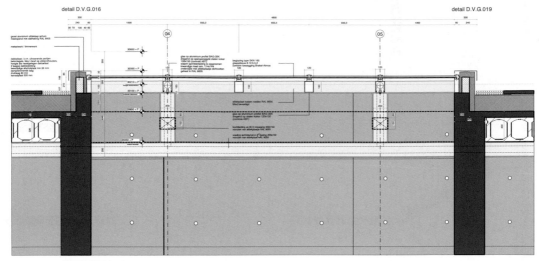

AANZICHT 6E003 (noord)

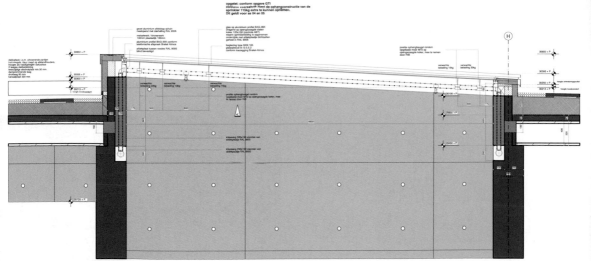

AANZICHT 6E019 spiegel (oost)

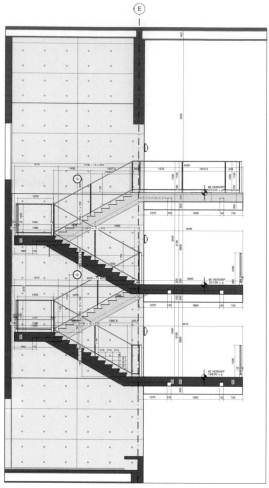

DOORSNEDE A

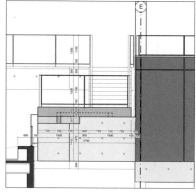

DOORSNEDE B

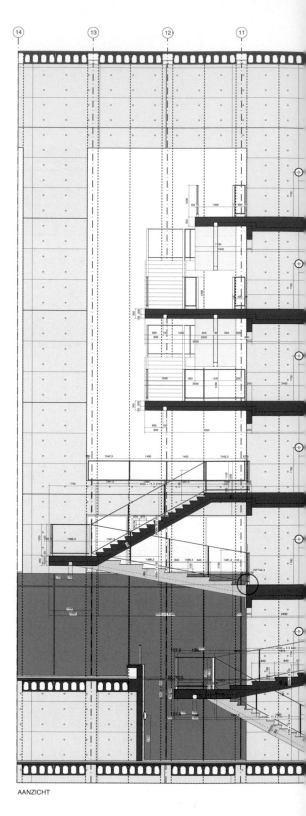

AANZICHT

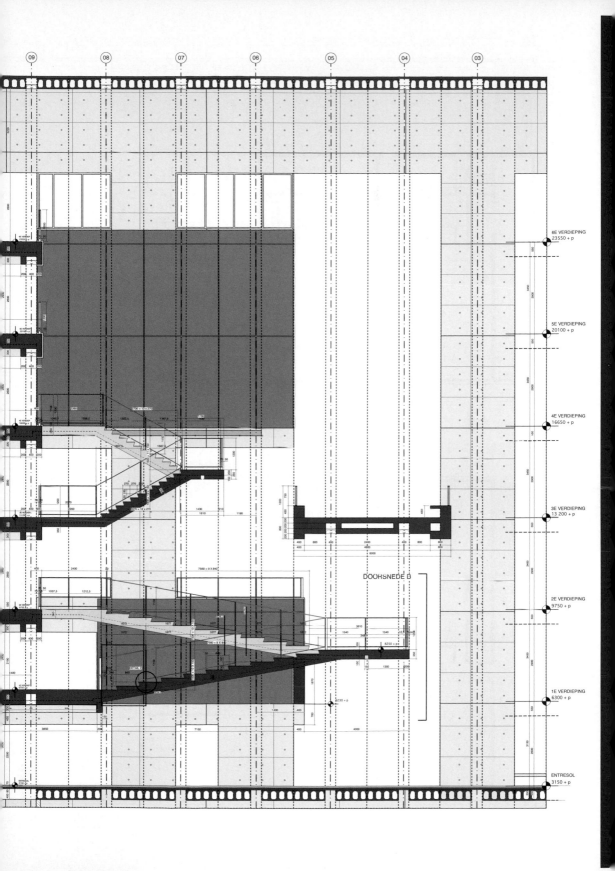

DOORSNEDE D

6E VERDIEPING
23550 + p

5E VERDIEPING
20100 + p

4E VERDIEPING
16650 + p

3E VERDIEPING
13 200 + p

2E VERDIEPING
9750 + p

1E VERDIEPING
6300 + p

ENTRESOL
3150 + p

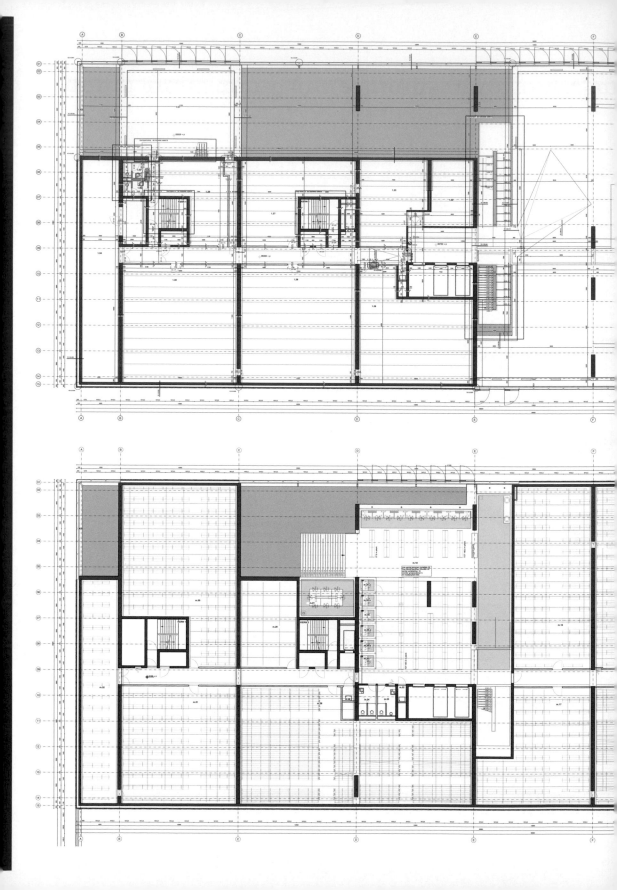

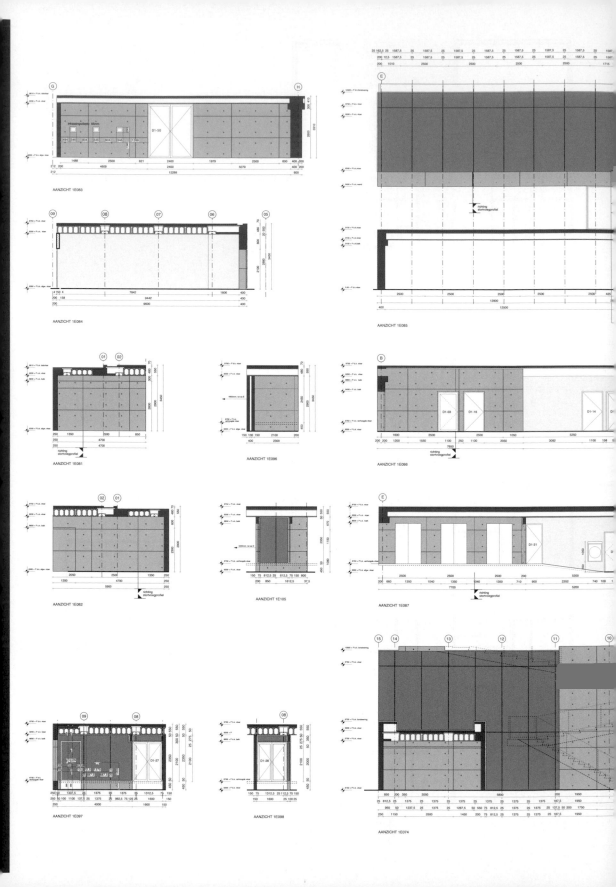

AANZICHT 1E083

AANZICHT 1E084

AANZICHT 1E085

AANZICHT 1E081

AANZICHT 1E096

AANZICHT 1E086

AANZICHT 1E082

AANZICHT 1E105

AANZICHT 1E087

AANZICHT 1E097

AANZICHT 1E098

AANZICHT 1E074

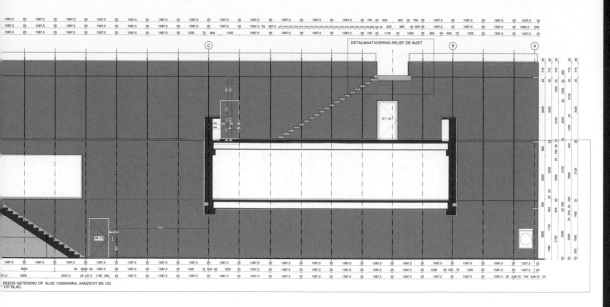

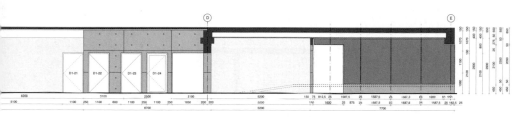

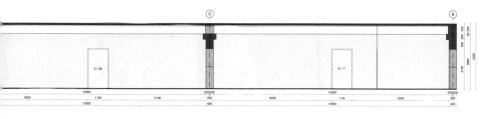

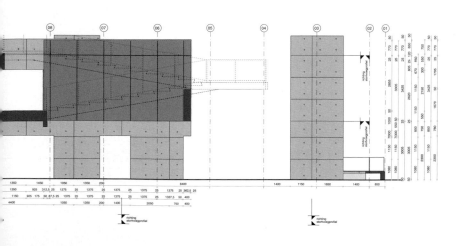

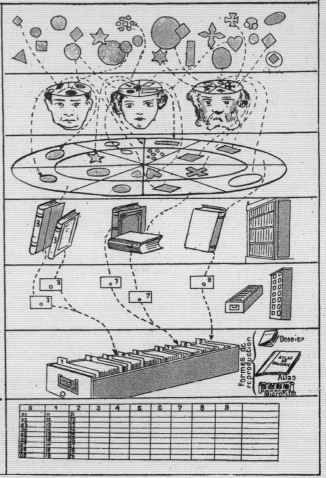

L'univers, l'intelligence, la science, le livre

Les choses

L'Univers, la Réalité, le Cosmos

Les intelligences

qui pensent les choses fragmentairement

La science

Remet et coordonne en ses cadres les pensées de toutes les intelligences particulières

Les Livres

Transcrivent et photographient la science selon l'ordre divisé des connaissances

La Collection de livres forment la Bibliothèque

La Bibliographie

Inventorie et catalogue les livres

La réunion de notices Bibliographiques forme le répertoire Bibliographique universel

L'Encyclopédie

(Texte et Image)

Dossier   Atlas   Microfilm

Concentre, classe et coordonne le contenu des livres

La Classification

Conforme à l'ordre que l'intelligence découvre dans les choses, sert à la fois à l'ordonnance de la science des livres, de leur Bibliographie et de l'Encyclopédie

0	1	2	3	4	5	6	7	8	9
01	11	21							
02	12	22							
03	13	23							
04	14	24							
05	15	25							
06	16	26							
07	17	27							
08	18	28							
09	19	29							

L'Univers, l'Intelligence, la Science, le Livre

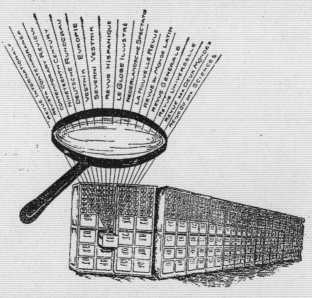

L'Encyclopédie documentaire.

Paul Otlet, Forefather of Information Architecture

Belgian lawyer, bibliographer, pacifist and entrepreneur Paul Otlet (1868-1944) set himself a utopian aim: establishing a database which would make all human knowledge accessible. The visionary, fanatical Otlet dedicated his life and spent his fortune on this idea. He wanted to make not only books accessible but also magazines, reports, brochures, newspapers and even visual material. In 1895 he founded the Institut International de Bibliographie, supported by the Belgian king, Leopold. Otlet's gigantic card system would come to stand not only in the Brussels Institute but copies of it would also be housed in other European capitals.

In 1910, in the wake of the Brussels World Fair, Otlet and his friend Henri LaFontaine created an installation La Répertoire Bibliographique Universel at the Palais Mondial. Originally envisioned as the centrepiece of a new 'city of intellect' this installation, called the Mundaneum was to be the hub of a utopian city that housed a society of the world's nations. A pacifist and an internationalist, Paul Otlet believed that shared knowledge and improved relations between peoples could lead to lasting peace. In 1914, he was one of the driving forces behind the League of Nations. By the outbreak of World War I, with the help of scores of staff, Otlet had managed to assemble 10 million cards. At Otlet's death in 1944, his life's work would consist of 12 million cards.

Taking the Dewey Decimal system as his starting point, Otlet began developing what came to be known as Universal Decimal Classification (UDC), now widely recognised as the first – and one of the only – full implementations of a faceted classification system. Otlet's retrieval system made it possible to divide larger units of information into smaller ones, by means of endless decimal positions. Related information could thus be meaningfully linked through the card system.

In the early 1930's Otlet began to speculate about how a wide range of then experimental technology – radio, cinema, microfilm, and television – could be combined to achieve a new complexity and variety of functionality in information searching, analysis, re-structuring and use. This set of functions he believed would eventually be embodied in new kinds of information machines that would be akin to what nowadays we have begun to call scholarly work stations.

His concluding prophetic description of an Ultimate Documentation Network is as follows:

'Everything in the universe, and everything of man, would be registered at a distance as it was produced. In this way a moving image of the world will be established, a true mirror of his memory. From a distance, everyone will be able to read text, enlarged and limited to the desired subject, projected on an individual screen. Everyone from his armchair will be able to contemplate creation, as a whole or in certain of its parts.'

Otlet turned out to be way ahead of his time. He became more and more entangled in his utopian plans and finally his whole house of cards, his 'world brain' collapsed. But Otlet's UDC classification system is still used all over the world. It is regarded today as similar to the hypertext that enables us to navigate through the computer network. His work is now seen as providing a very broad-based introduction to important aspects of modern information science. And Otlet himself, forgotten now for a long time, has been rediscovered as the forefather of information architecture.

Paul Otlet, Monde: essaie d'universalisme - connaissance du monde; sentiment du monde; action organisée et plan du monde, Brussels, Editions du Mundaneum, 1935, pp. 390-391
Paul Otlet, Traité de documentation; le livre sur le livre: théorie et pratique, 1934
Schneiders, P., Nederlandse bibliotheekgeschiedenis, van librije tot virtuele bibliotheek, Den Haag 1997, pp. 218-221
Wright, A., Forgotten Forefather: Paul Otlet,
www.boxesandarrows.com/archives/forgotten_forefather_paul_otlet.php
(last accessed 3 January 2005)

PERSPECTIVES WITH A PIRANESIAN DIMENSION

Utrecht University was founded in 1636. In the 1960s, as in so many other European cities, it was decided to build a new campus. De Uithof was constructed east of Utrecht on an open tract of land divided by straight avenues that bear the names of European university cities. In 1986 OMA/Rem Koolhaas was commissioned to draw up an urban master plan to be implemented in phases. The plan involved building along both sides of Heidelberglaan. A number of striking buildings were completed in the 1990s, among them the Educatorium by OMA/Rem Koolhaas and the Minnaert building by Neutelings Riedijk Architects. Art Zaaijer Architects supervised the implementation of the OMA plan for the campus. A central argument for building the new library on the urban axis was to create a raised walkway connection to the adjoining campus buildings.

The Wiel Arets commission was two-part: to design a library and car park for 450 vehicles. The subdivision is radical: a garden extends the entire length, and a small café is located on the outermost flank. The structure of the car park has been calculated to accommodate a possible extension to the book depot above.

The spare rectangular volume betrays nothing of the building's remarkable interior. The only clue to the outstanding interior composition is the interplay of concrete and glass panels on the façade. The concrete areas mark the depots, book depositories that are closed to the public. Both the glass and concrete façade panels have been screen printed with a willow pattern based on a Kim Zwarts photograph. Rubber moulds were used to create a relief effect on the prefabricated concrete panels, while the interior concrete walls were poured on site. The concrete walls in relief mark the location of the book depositories. The screen print on the glass also lends the interior a constantly changing atmosphere thanks to the fluctuating intensity of incoming sunlight. On cloudy days the pattern is softer, becoming sharper and clearer as the light brightens. The glazed sections, graded from top to bottom, also create a striking effect. The patterned glass also makes allowances for the amount of daylight admission required by libraries. The façade has been structurally bonded, something quite remarkable in the Netherlands given the extremely strict technical standards demanded. A number of glass panels can be opened for an unobstructed view.

The basic structure comprises twenty columns and four fixed cores, which is a considerable feat of construction. The reading rooms are attached to the huge depositories. Arets opted for finishes that were true to the structure wherever possible, so there are no low ceilings to conceal technical installations. Spaces measuring 40 by 40 centimetres were created between the long vaults to houses both the lighting system and sprinkler installation. This called for precise proportions throughout the building. The different depots together can accommodate a total of 104.5 kilometres of bookshelves. Books are transported between the various depots by central chutes that are connected to one another at basement level.

A great deal of thought went into the way people enter the building. There is no immediate view of the interior – even the staircases are located off the axis leading from the doors. A mezzanine with auditorium is located between the lobby and main reception desk at precisely the point where the staircase narrows and the construction changes. This is the point where a breathtakingly tall, cavernous void rises through the building. From the reception desk on the first floor the main staircase winds up through the tall central space. Considerable attention was given to the structure of the staircase, which provides access to each level. The openness results in unexpected, provocative perspectives that are Piranesian in character. On the double-height top floor the most valuable books and documents are stored. All the technical installations are built into the thickness of the roof to leave a clean, uncluttered roof surface.

Arets settled on black for the ceiling and walls to lend the interior a distinct character. The floor finish is a glossy grey. The white tables and books are the central feature of the library. All counters and lounge seating in the raised walkway have a bright red covering – the only colour besides the books and visitors' clothing. Thorough research into artificial lighting was needed to perfect the colour scheme.

Within the Dutch context, this is an extraordinary structure. While many architects focus on conceptual design and leave building to technical offices, Arets is resolute in keeping both elements of the process intact. A tight-knit team studied every aspect of implementation, right down to the tiniest detail. This is how Arets achieved a meticulously detailed building without recourse to standard details. That said, this concept called for impeccable craftsmanship and coordination skills. The extended period of preparation from initial idea through to construction certainly helped the architects to manage the enormously complex schedule of requirements and translate it into a building with a complex spatial configuration. Separating the depositories and reading rooms gives the library a spectacular atmosphere rarely found in buildings of this type. In the library construction sector, this is a truly exceptional building.

Marc Dubois

The Library Hotel

The Library Hotel, New York, is set at the corner of Madison Avenue and 41st. Street near the New York City Public Library and the Pierpont Morgan Library. Each of the ten guestroom floors of the Library Hotel is dedicated to one of the ten major categories of the Dewey Decimal System: Social Sciences, Literature, Languages, History, Math & Science, General Knowledge, Technology, Philosophy, The Arts and Religion. Each of the sixty exquisitely appointed accommodations has been individually adorned with a collection of art and books relevant to one distinctive topic within the category of floor it belongs to.

Library Hotel
www.libraryhotel.com
(last accessed 6 January 2005)

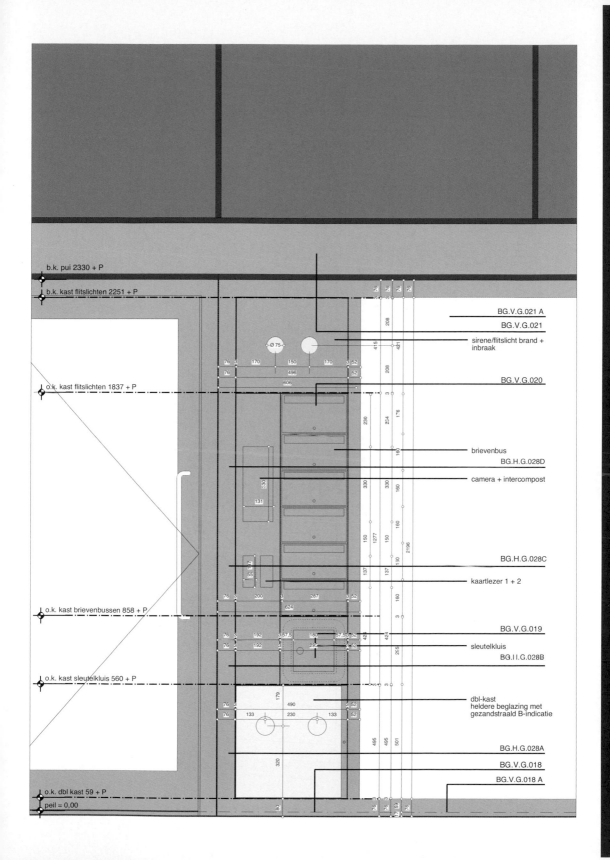

b.k. pui 2330 + P

b.k. kast flitslichten 2251 + P

BG.V.G.021 A

BG.V.G.021

sirene/flitslicht brand +
inbraak

Ø 75

76 170 150 170 52

76 496 52

606

o.k. kast flitslichten 1837 + P

BG.V.G.020

230 254 176

brievenbus

BG.H.G.028D

330 330 160

camera + intercompost

131

150 1277 150 160

2196

BG.H.G.028C

137 137 130

kaartlezer 1 + 2

55

76 200 287 52

624

o.k. kast brievenbussen 858 + P

BG.V.G.019

76 192 57.5 180 57.5 52 423 424

sleutelkluis

76 192 52 255

BG.II.G.028B

o.k. kast sleutelkluis 560 + P

179

dbl-kast
heldere beglazing met
gezandstraald B-indicatie

76 490 52

76 133 230 133 52

495 495 501

BG.H.G.028A

320

BG.V.G.018

BG.V.G.018 A

o.k. dbl kast 59 + P

peil = 0,00

80

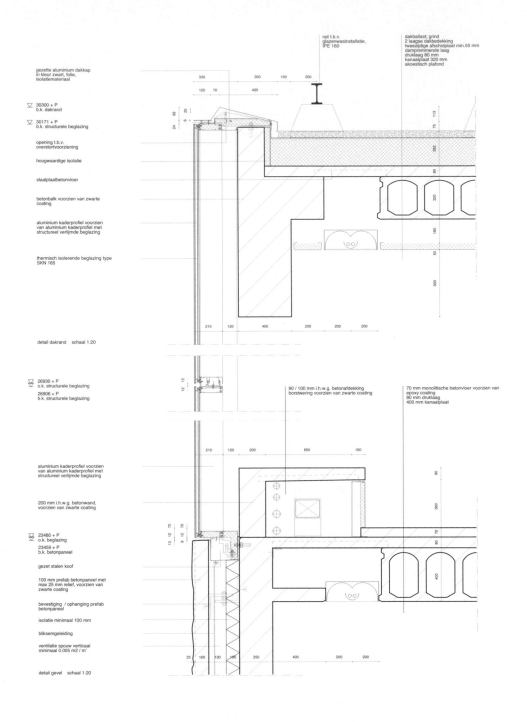

gezette aluminium dakkap
in kleur zwart, folie,
isolatiemateriaal

▽ 30300 + P
b.k. dakrand

▽ 30171 + P
b.k. structurele beglazing

opening t.b.v.
overstortvoorziening

hoogwaardige isolatie

staalplaatbetonvloer

betonbalk voorzien van zwarte
coating

aluminium kaderprofiel voorzien
van aluminium kaderprofiel met
structureel verlijmde beglazing

thermisch isolerende beglazing type
SKN 165

detail dakrand   schaal 1:20

rail t.b.v.
glazenwasinstallatie,
IPE 160

dakballast; grind
2 laagse dakbedekking
tweezijdige afschotplaat min.50 mm
dampremmende laag
druklaag 80 mm
kanaalplaat 320 mm
akoestisch plafond

330   300   100   200

125   70   435

▽ 26930 + P
o.k. structurele beglazing

26906 + P
b.k. structurele beglazing

90 / 100 mm i.h.w.g. betonafdekking
borstwering voorzien van zwarte coating

70 mm monolitische betonvloer voorzien van
epoxy coating
80 mm druklaag
400 mm kanaalplaat

aluminium kaderprofiel voorzien
van aluminium kaderprofiel met
structureel verlijmde beglazing

200 mm i.h.w.g. betonwand,
voorzien van zwarte coating

▽ 23480 + P
o.k. beglazing

23459 + P
b.k. betonpaneel

gezet stalen koof

100 mm prefab betonpaneel met
max 25 mm relief, voorzien van
zwarte coating

bevestiging / ophanging prefab
betonpaneel

isolatie minimaal 100 mm

bliksemgeleiding

ventilatie spouw verticaal
minimaal 0.005 m2 / m'

detail gevel   schaal 1:20

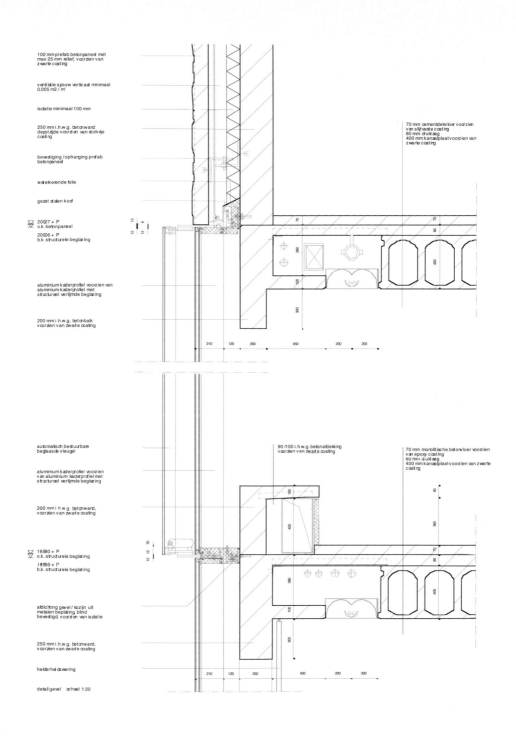

100 mm prefab betonpaneel met
max 25 mm relief, voorzien van
zwarte coating

ventilatie spouw verticaal minimaal
0.005 m2 / m²

isolatie minimaal 100 mm

250 mm i.h.w.g. betonwand
dezetzijde voorzien van stofvrije
coating

bevestiging /opharging prefab
betonpaneel

waterkerende folie

gezet stalen koof

20027 + P
o.k. betonpaneel
20006 + P
b.k. structurele beglazing

aluminium kaderprofiel voorzien van
aluminium kaderprofiel met
structureel verlijmde beglazing

200 mm i.h.w.g. betonbalk
voorzien van zwarte coating

70 mm cementdekvloer voorzien
van slijtvaste coating
80 mm druklaag
400 mm kanaalplaat voorzien van
zwarte coating

automatisch bestuurbare
beglaasde vleugel

aluminium kaderprofiel voorzien
van aluminium kaderprofiel met
structureel verlijmde beglazing

200 mm i.h.w.g. betonwand,
voorzien van zwarte coating

16590 + P
o.k. structurele beglazing
16560 + P
b.k. structurele beglazing

afdichting gevel / kozijn uit
metalen beplating, blind
bevestigd, voorzien van isolatie

250 mm i.h.w.g. betonwand,
voorzien van zwarte coating

helderheidswering

detail gevel schaal 1:20

90 /100 i.h.w.g. betonafdekking
voorzien van zwarte coating

70 mm monolitische betonvloer voorzien
van epoxy coating
80 mm druklaag
400 mm kanaalplaat voorzien van zwarte
coating

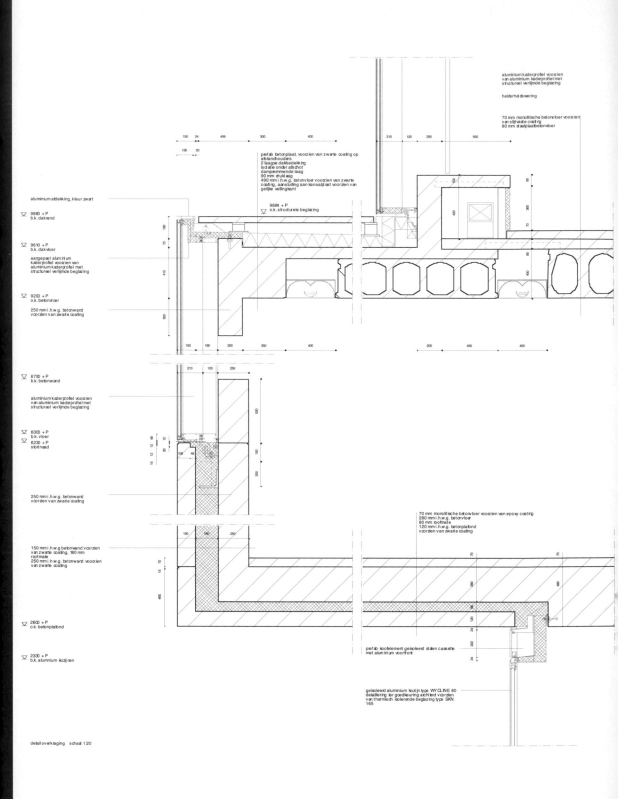

aluminium kaderprofiel voorzien
van aluminium kaderprofiel met
structureel verlijmde beglazing

helderheidswering

70 mm monolitische betonvloer voorzien
van slijtvaste coating
80 mm staalplaatbetonvloer

aluminium afdekking, kleur zwart

prefab betonplaat, voorzien van zwarte coating op
afstandhouders
2 laagse dakbedekking
isolatie onder afschot
dampremmende laag
90 mm drukllaag
490 mm i.h.w.g. betonvloer voorzien van zwarte
coating, aansluiting aan kanaalplaat voorzien van
gelijke vellingkant

9860 + P
b.k. dakrand

9884 + P
o.k. structurele beglazing

9610 + P
b.k. dakvloer

aangepast aluminium
kaderprofiel voorzien van
aluminium kaderprofiel met
structureel verlijmde beglazing

9200 + P
o.k. betonvloer

250 mm i.h.w.g. betonwand
voorzien van zwarte coating

6750 + P
b.k. betonwand

aluminium kaderprofiel voorzien
van aluminium kaderprofiel met
structureel verlijmde beglazing

6300 + P
b.k. vloer
6230 + P
stortnaad

250 mm i.h.w.g. betonwand
voorzien van zwarte coating

70 mm monolitische betonvloer voorzien van epoxy coating
280 mm i.h.w.g. betonvloer
80 mm roofmate
120 mm i.h.w.g. betonplafond
voorzien van zwarte coating

150 mm i.h.w.g. betonwand voorzien
van zwarte coating, 180 mm
roofmate
250 mm i.h.w.g. betonwand voorzien
van zwarte coating

2600 + P
o.k. betonplafond

2330 + P
b.k. aluminium kozijnen

prefab koofelement geisoleerd stalen cassette
met aluminium voorfront

geisoleerd aluminium kozijn type WYCLINE 60
detaillering ter goedkeuring architect voorzien
van thermisch isolerende beglazing type SKN
165

detail overkraging   schaal 1:20

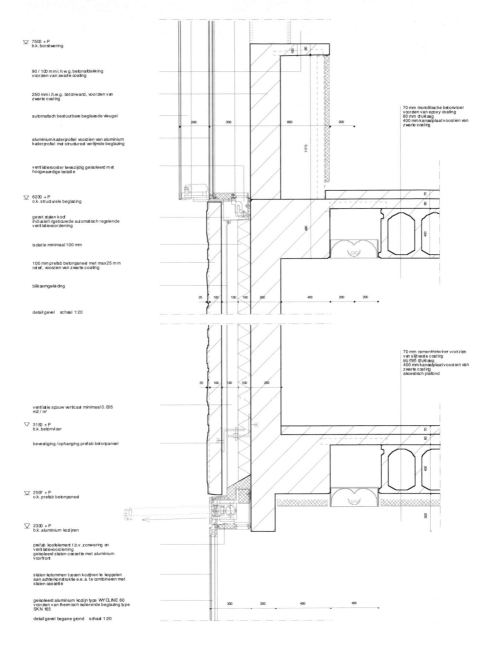

▽ 7500 +P
b.k.borstwering

90 / 100 mm i.h.w.g. betonafdekking
voorzien van zwarte coating

250 mm i.h.w.g. betonrand, voorzien van
zwarte coating

automatisch bestuurbare beglaasde vleugel

aluminium kaderprofiel voorzien van aluminium
kaderprofiel met structureel verlijmde beglazing

ventilatierooster tweezijdig geïsoleerd met
hoogwaardige isolatie

▽ 6230 +P
o.k. structurele beglazing

gezet stalen kopf
inclusief ingebouwde automatisch regelende
ventilatievoorziening

isolatie minimaal 100 mm

100 mm prefab betonpaneel met max 25 mm
relief, voorzien van zwarte coating

bliksemgeleiding

detail gevel   schaal 1:20

ventilatie spouw verticaal minimaal 0.005
m2 / m²

▽ 3150 +P
b.k.betonvloer

bevestiging / opharging prefab betonpaneel

▽ 2597 +P
o.k. prefab betonpaneel

▽ 2330 +P
b.k. aluminium kozijnen

prefab koofelement t.b.v. zonwering en
ventilatievoorziening
geïsoleerd stalen cassette met aluminium
voorfront

stalen kolommen tussen kozijnen te koppelen
aan achterkonstruktie e.e.a. te combineren met
stalen cassette

geïsoleerd aluminium kozijn type WICLINE 60
voorzien van thermisch isolererde beglazing type
SKN 165

detail gevel begane grond   schaal 1:20

70 mm monolitische betonvloer
voorzien van epoxy coating
80 mm drukläag
400 mm kanaalplaat voorzien van
zwarte coating

70 mm cementdekvloer voorzien
van slijtvaste coating
80 mm drukläag
400 mm kanaalplaat voorzien van
zwarte coating
akoestisch plafond

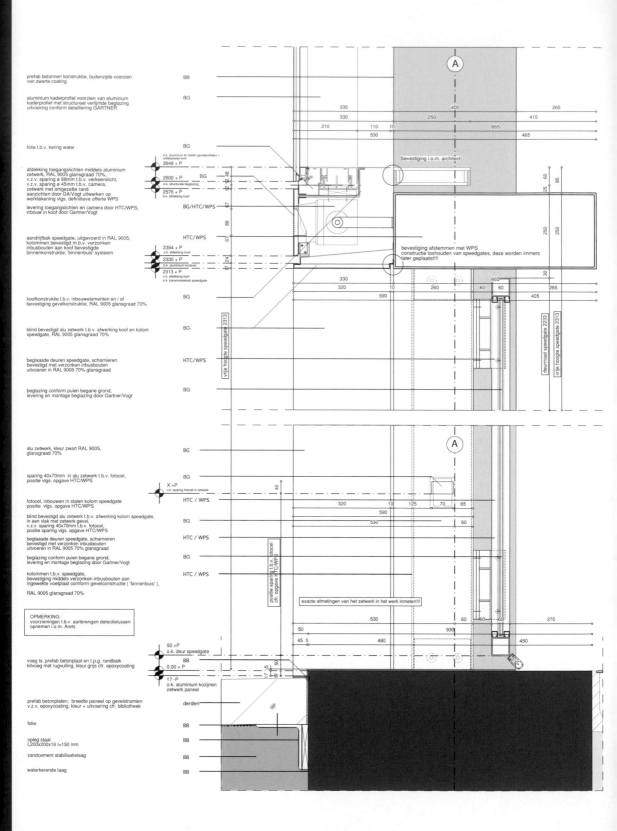

prefab betonnen konstruktie, buitenzijde voorzien van zwarte coating

aluminium kaderprofiel voorzien van aluminium kaderprofiel met structureel verlijmde beglazing uitvoering conform detaillering GARTNER

folie t.b.v. kering water

afdekking toegangslichten middels aluminium zetwerk, RAL 9005 glansgraad 70%, v.z.v. sparing ø 88mm t.b.v. verkeerslicht, v.z.v. sparing ø 45mm t.b.v. camera, zetwerk met omgezette rand aanzichten door GA/Vogt uitwerken op werktekening vlgs. definitieve offerte WPS

levering toegangslichten en camera door HTC/WPS, inbouw in koof door Gartner/Vogt,

aandrijfbak speedgate, uitgevoerd in RAL 9005, kolommen bevestigd m.b.v. verzonken inbusbouten aan koof bevestigde binnenkonstruktie, 'binnenbuis' systeem

koofkonstruktie t.b.v. inbouwelementen en / of bevestiging gevelkonstruktie, RAL 9005 glansgraad 70%

blind bevestigd alu zetwerk t.b.v. afwerking koof en kolom speedgate, RAL 9005 glansgraad 70%

beglaasde deuren speedgate, scharnieren bevestigd met verzonken inbusbouten uitvoeren in RAL 9005 70% glansgraad

beglazing conform puien begane grond, levering en montage beglazing door Gartner/Vogt

alu zetwerk, kleur zwart RAL 9005, glansgraad 70%

sparing 40x70mm in alu zetwerk t.b.v. fotocel, positie vlgs. opgave HTC/WPS

fotocel, inbouwen in stalen kolom speedgate positie vlgs. opgave HTC/WPS

blind bevestigd alu zetwerk t.b.v. afwerking kolom speedgate, in een vlak met zetwerk gevel, v.z.v. sparing 40x70mm t.b.v. fotocel, positie sparing vlgs. opgave HTC/WPS

beglaasde deuren speedgate, scharnieren bevestigd met verzonken inbusbouten uitvoeren in RAL 9005 70% glansgraad

beglazing conform puien begane grond, levering en montage beglazing door Gartner/Vogt

kolommen t.b.v. speedgate, bevestiging middels verzonken inbusbouten aan ingewekte voetplaat comform gevelconstructie ('binnenbuis'),

RAL 9005 glansgraad 70%

OPMERKING:
voorzieningen t.b.v. aanbrengen detectielussen opnemen i.o.m. Arets

voeg ts. prefab betonplaat en t.p.g. randbalk kitvoeg met rugvulling, kleur grijs cfr. epoxycoating

prefab betonplaten, breedte paneel op gevelstramien v.z.v. epoxycoating, kleur + uitvoering cfr. bibliotheek

folie

oplegstaal L200x200x16 l=150 mm

zandcement stabilisatielaag

waterkerende laag

BB
BG
BG
2648 + P — b.k. aluminium en stalen gevelprofielen + afdekplaatje koof
2600 + P — b.k. structurele beglazing
2576 + P — b.k. afdekking koof
BG/HTC/WPS
HTC/WPS
2354 + P — b.k. aluminium kozijnen
2330 + P — b.k. afdekking koof
2313 + P — o.k. transmissiekast speedgate
BG
BG
HTC/WPS
BG
BG
BG
X +P — o.k. sparing fotocel in zetwerk
HTC / WPS
BG
HTC / WPS
BG
HTC / WPS
50 +P — o.k. deur speedgate
BB
0.00 = P
17 -P — o.k. aluminium kozijnen zetwerk paneel
derden
BB
BB
BB
BB

bevestiging i.o.m. architect

bevestiging afstemmen met WPS constructie loshouden van speedgates, deze worden immers later geplaatst!!!

exacte afmetingen van het zetwerk in het werk inmeten!!!

positie sparing t.b.v. fotocel cfr. opgave HTC/WPS

vrije hoogte speedgate 2313

deurmaat speedgate 2233

vrije hoogte speedgate 2313

330 400 265
330 250 415
210 110 10 665
530 465
60 85
25 250
250
330 665 30
320 10 260 60 60 285
590 405
40
320 10 125 70 65
590
530 60
530 60 60 270
930
50 45 5 480 450

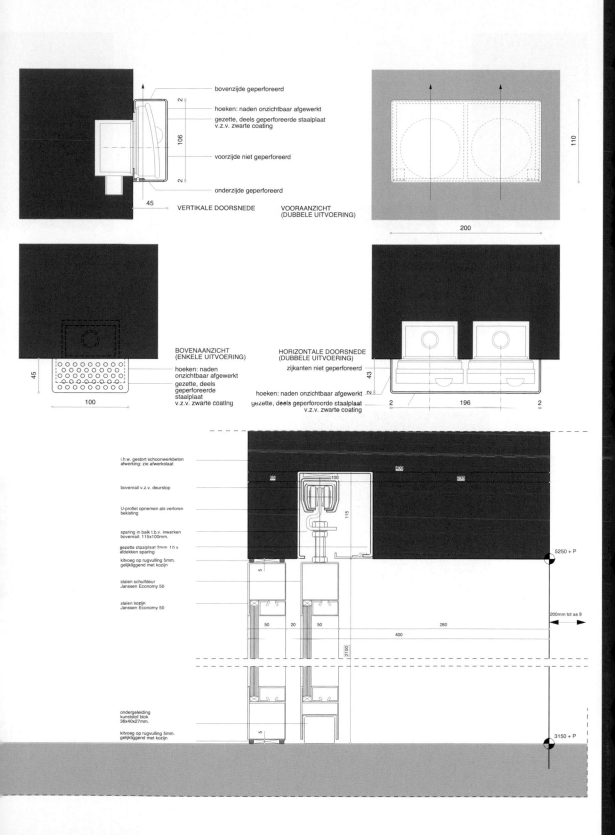

bovenzijde geperforeerd

hoeken: naden onzichtbaar afgewerkt

gezette, deels geperforeerde staalplaat
v.z.v. zwarte coating

voorzijde niet geperforeerd

onderzijde geperforeerd

2

106

2

45

VERTIKALE DOORSNEDE

VOORAANZICHT
(DUBBELE UITVOERING)

110

200

45

100

BOVENAANZICHT
(ENKELE UITVOERING)

hoeken: naden
onzichtbaar afgewerkt

gezette, deels
geperforeerde
staalplaat
v.z.v. zwarte coating

HORIZONTALE DOORSNEDE
(DUBBELE UITVOERING)

zijkanten niet geperforeerd

43

hoeken: naden onzichtbaar afgewerkt

gezette, deels geperforeerde staalplaat
v.z.v. zwarte coating

2   196   2

i.h.w. gestort schoonwerkbeton
afwerking: zie afwerkstaat

bovenrail v.z.v. deurstop

U-profiel opnemen als verloren
bekisting

sparing in balk t.b.v. inwerken
bovenrail: 115x100mm.

gezette staalplaat 2mm t.b.v
afdekken sparing

kitvoeg op rugvulling 5mm.
gelijkliggend met kozijn

stalen schuifdeur
Janssen Economy 50

stalen kozijn
Janssen Economy 50

ondergeleiding
kunststof blok
36x40x27mm.

kitvoeg op rugvulling 5mm.
gelijkliggend met kozijn

100

115

5

5

50   20   50   280

400

2100

5250 + P

200mm tot as 9

3150 + P

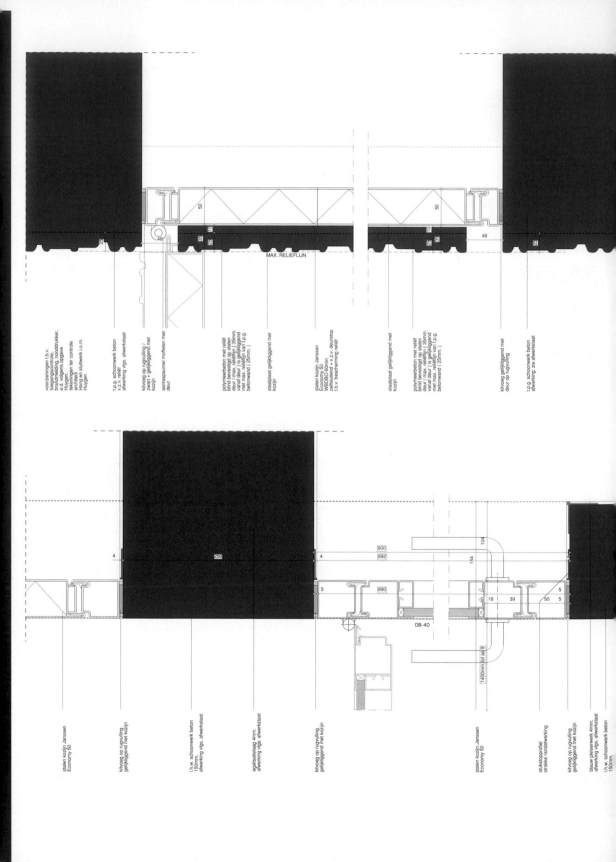

MAX. RELIEFLIJN

voorzieningen t.b.v.
toegangscontrole,
brandmelding, noodrukker,
e.d. volgens opgave
Huygen,
tekeningen ter controle
architect
Hang en sluitwerk i.o.m.
Huygen

t.p.g. schoonwerk beton
v.z.v. reliëf
afwerking vlgs. afwerkstaat

kitvoeg op rugvulling /
zwart + gelijkliggend met
kozijn

aanslagpaumel moffelen met
deur

polymeerbeton met reliëf
blind bevestigd op stalen
deur / max. reliëflijn (35mm.
vanaf deur) is gelijkliggend
met max. reliëflijn van t.p.g.
betonwand (25mm.)

staalplaat gelijkliggend met
kozijn

stalen kozijn Janssen
Economy 50
WBDBO 60min
zelfsluitend + v.z.v. deurstop
t.b.v. bescherming reliëf

staalplaat gelijkliggend met
kozijn

polymeerbeton met reliëf
blind bevestigd op stalen
deur / max. reliëflijn (35mm.
vanaf deur) is gelijkliggend
met max. reliëflijn van t.p.g.
betonwand (25mm.)

kitvoeg gelijkliggend met
deur op rugvulling

t.p.g. schoonwerk beton
afwerking: zie afwerkstaat

stalen kozijn
Economy 50

kitvoeg op rugvulling
gelijkliggend met kozijn

i.h.w. schoonwerk beton
150mm.
afwerking vlgs. afwerkstaat

egalisatielaag 4mm.
afwerking vlgs. afwerkstaat

kitvoeg op rugvulling
gelijkliggend met kozijn

stalen kozijn Janssen
Economy 50

stukstopprofiel
strakke randafwerking

kitvoeg op rugvulling
gelijkliggend met kozijn

blauw pleisterwerk 4mm.
afwerking vlgs. afwerkstaat

i.h.w. schoonwerk beton
150mm.

DB-40

1400mm tot as

A Burial Chamber for Murdered Books

Under the Berlin Bebelplatz lies one of the most impressive memories of the Nazi dictatorship: a library with empty shelves. This monument designed by the Israeli artist Micha Ullman has, since 1995, commemorated the living memory of the book-burnings that took place here – on the square in front of the Humboldt University – on May 10, 1933. There is no access to the cube-shaped space. It can only be seen through a glass-plate in the paving of the square. And even then the glass-plate never reveals more than a slice of the space below. The austere artwork refers to the loss and vulnerability of our cultural heritage. It derives its power among other things from its restraint. The underground, brightly lit space leaves the square itself entirely unaffected.

In 2004 a car park was constructed under the whole Bebelplatz. A storm of protest from opponents, including the president of the international writers organisation PEN György Konrád, has been of no avail. Konrad, who described the monument as 'a burial chamber for murdered books', and his supporters believed that this intervention would violate the monument. The 'Bibliothek' or 'Das Mahnmal' itself has been preserved, but underground it is now completely surrounded by the garage.

Freie Universität Berlin
http://userpage.fu-berlin.de/~sampras/buecher/mahnm.htm
(last accessed 14 September 2004)
Wöhr+Bauer Gmbh
www.woehrbauer.de/de/index_de.html
(last accessed 5 January 2005)

Für immer verloren?

...ch dem Brand in de...
...na Amalia Bibliothe...

Human Chain to Rescue Books

In a fire at the Anna Amalia Library, one of Germany's most historic libraries, up to 30,000 irreplaceable books were destroyed. In September 2004 the library with Germany's most beautiful Library Hall, situated in the eastern city of Weimar, was caught by a blaze.

Among the literary treasures lost in the library were thousands of works from the 16th to 18th centuries, including the sheet music archive of the library's patron, Anna Amalia (1739-1807), the Duchess of Saxony-Weimar and 10,000 original editions of Shakespeare's works. Another 40,000 books were damaged by the smoke and water used by the firefighters.

Some 120,000 books, including a 1534 Bible once owned by Martin Luther, were saved when the library's staff, firefighters and more than 100 Weimar residents formed a human chain to rescue them. They also managed rescue the world's largest collection of copies of Goethe's Faust.

The market value of the books damaged and destroyed could not be estimated exactly because they were unique and uninsured. A sum of 20 million euro has been calculated to restore the entire collection.

Lost Forever? After the fire in the Anna Amalia Library from: TV programme
'Rettung für Weimars Kulturerbe' (Rescue for Weimars cultural heritage),
Mitteldeutscher Rundfunk, 2004

AGOL Terminal and Computerised Catalogues

In 1975 a 'terminal' was set up in the Utrecht University Library: a large blue machine with a modem and telephone. By means of a complicated wire connection it was possible to make contact with America, where the actual computer was located. The terminal enabled the consultation of major international subject bibliographies such as Chemical Abstracts, Biological Abstracts or Psychological Abstracts. To make use of this - at the time ultramodern - service, academic staff could fill in a special application form at their faculty and then make an appointment with a staff member of the university library who would carry out the 'search'. If the connection was successful, files were searched using keywords from a thesaurus in an interactive process. The brochure Looking for Sources with the Computer reads: 'it is as if one is in dialogue with the computer'. The end product, a list of relevant titles and abstracts, was printed in America and usually reached Utrecht through the post after about ten days. The room with the blue terminal radiated a spirit of innovation. The most well-known 'host institutions' at that time were Lockheed in California and Dimdi in Germany. In Utrecht AGOL, Afdeling Geautomatiseerde Ontsluiting van Literatuur or Department for Automated Access to Literature was set up to provide this service. Recent developments in the computerisation of catalogues mean that users now have ample opportunity for searching through catalogues in various ways and achieving better results more quickly.

Of course these new technical possibilities are not limited to the traditional collection of 'paper' books and journals in libraries. The collections in libraries nowadays also consist of (access to) a large number of digital sources of information: from journal articles to digitised versions of 'paper publications' as well as the gigantic amount of information which can be found on the internet.

When the library was first computerised the way in which a search was carried out and the presentation of results were often an exact copy of the way in which information was kept in the old card index catalogue known as the Leiden booklets. These days the user can search in computerised catalogues using almost any element of a title description, often combining a number of elements as well.

Daan Thoomes, Gerard Baltussen, Utrecht University Library

300

THE LIVING ROOM OF THE UNIVERSITY
Dialogue Aryan Sikkema and Art Zaaijer

Has the UBU as a building become what you, as 'guardians' of De Uithof campus as a whole, had expected or hoped it would be?

Aryan Sikkema: The library is becoming a meeting place, a sort of living room for De Uithof and hopefully for the university as a whole. Even on Sunday there are now more students sitting here than in the city centre. The more people hear about this fantastic building the busier it will become. A sense of pride and identity among staff and students is what we are looking for. And the library certainly contributes to this.

Art Zaaijer: Now the library is there everything will turn out alright for De Uithof. The area has gained a heart; the library is the keystone in the centre. As far as compactness of building and programmatic richness are concerned De Uithof now has a clarity that, I believe, can never be lost.

How did De Uithof actually develop into the area it is now?

AS: When I started working here at the end of 1984 De Uithof was an inhospitable area with a building standing haphazardly here or there. The university wanted to change that so we asked Rem Koolhaas's OMA to present a vision of the future of the campus.

AZ: I've been working on this since the beginning. In this vision the landscape is the greatest asset, an asset we didn't want to waste. The landscape structure was intended to separate the buildings from one another and at the same time link them together.

AS: OMA's underlying principle for this was that the historical waterways and old dykes were based on a mainly diagonal structure while the buildings from the 1960s and '70s were rectangular. OMA wanted to adhere to this principle, which had emerged over time, of 'new is right-angled and old is diagonal'. Clashes between old and new could moreover produce interesting moments from a spatial point of view. And that is what you now see.

What else was included in the urban development plan?

AZ: We decided to define clusters measuring 1.5 by 2 kilometres within that enormous terrain. Within each cluster anything is possible, as long as a few simple rules are respected. Nothing is allowed outside it. The borders of the clusters have been drawn on the map since 1988 and so nothing has changed there. The more that is built within the cluster borders, which are relatively strict and limited, the nearer the buildings will naturally be to each other. In the central cluster this means that the buildings are built literally up against one another. So that is the aim: direct proximity, but then on the basis of good neighbourliness. The buildings are individuals, but they stand next to each other without any ado, one dressed in casual clothes, the next in a suit and tie. The neighbourliness generates interaction. Not only between the buildings themselves, but – even more importantly – between their users. They start to share facilities and you get mixed functions and double ground use.

The best example of this is the Kashba zone in the central area where an additional rule applies. When a candidate comes forward for a 'slice' of a cluster we ask how many square metres are needed. We then give half this amount as a development plot. The higher they build the more space there will be for patios and so on. This also means that the corner of the slice has to be built on in such a way that the neighbour can fit next to it perfectly. The buildings are thus literally pushed together. So a massive block of buildings is created which is only broken internally. There are no alleys between the buildings but there are patios and internal pathways.

Did the urban development plan stipulate which functions should come where?

AZ: No, we fixed nothing to do with that. Luckily we did not allow ourselves to be swayed by the fashion for programming current at that time because functional demands are always changing. You can't go running after them; decisions like that need to be left to the common-sense of the moment. That principle, in our opinion, has formed the background for the mixture of functions which is now emerging. One cluster now consists, for example, of three faculty buildings, a library, a car park, another faculty building, housing and another university structure. As far as we are concerned that's marvellous. That's what you want a campus to be.

AS: Originally only university buildings were located in De Uithof. Later they were joined by the faculties and by businesses with close links to De Uithof. Now there are shops, sports facilities, hotels and restaurants, and other amenities, with the recent addition of housing. We have built 1000 student rooms and more will follow. This accommodation is a great success, although everyone was fiercely opposed to it until ten years ago. At the moment we are busy making the campus even more attractive by further reducing its monofunctional character, which brings with it too many risks for the long-term quality of the area.

De Uithof should become a multifunctional area, a satellite of the city of Utrecht. A place you go to even when you're not studying.

When and why was it decided to move the Central University Library to De Uithof?

AS: The decision to move the Central Library from the city centre to De Uithof was a major decision. The university's centre of gravity had gradually shifted to De Uithof. So we wanted to provide the students with a suitable place there for studying, reading rooms, independent work, discussion and so on. Of course we weren't sure it would work, but moving the library fits in well with the policy of turning De Uithof into a fully-fledged multifunctional centre. The idea of having the library in its current position was in fact in Koolhaas's earliest plan.
AZ: Against all principles we always kept the plot where the library now stands free in case the library would move to De Uithof. If the decision was ever finally made, then we wanted to be able to offer the best site at the heart of De Uithof. That is why we allowed a gap in the building developments for six to eight years to keep that plot free.

How does the design of the library relate to De Uithof as a whole?

AZ: Wiel's design has an entirely convincing clarity. The site now houses an unambiguous and complete entity comprising a car park, patio, and of course the library itself – very decided and very strong. Another good point is the way in which the library is elevated on a plinth, along an important pedestrian axis. That plinth will contain shops and a café. It is a very powerful block, an example of a building with a special aura, without frills. Bang! Another block, as strong as the Minnaert building. And then you can see how block architecture can result in a very good building.
The library is modest on the outside; it doesn't manifest itself through complexity of form. Instead, the building's charm is to be found on the inside. Within, you find yourself in a sort of treasure chamber. From the outside the library is beautiful and respectable, but inside it's velvety and glistening. The library will be vital to the image of De Uithof for the coming two centuries.
A building like this, if well-designed, can last for 200 years. If you design it badly it'll be flattened in thirty years, and if very badly in twenty years. That's why for an assignment like this you need an architect who can cope with the weight of the task.
AS: In my opinion Wiel Arets has achieved with the university library what we also want to achieve with the landscape in De Uithof: wide perspectives and great spaciousness combined with intimacy. Only the scale is different.
The new university library gives students and staff at the University of Utrecht a sense of pride that they can work and be here. The library gives identity to the location, to the surroundings, to the campus, and also to the city of Utrecht.
Users' reactions so far have varied from positive to "it's unbelievable that this is possible". Students are amazed at the stylish chairs and beautiful computers. A comfortable interior is something which we indeed find to be important. And buying in bulk means of course that you can insist on a lower price. I think that the building will soon become so loved by its users that it will acquire a lasting character on account of that alone.

What will the function of the library be in twenty or thirty years time?

AS: That question is hard to answer. Of course there will always be a need to preserve books as cultural heritage. And people will still need a place to study quietly, even if they bring their own books and laptop with them. That place, and an attractive place, they can find here. There will still be a need for a place to work together with others. And the need remains for a place where one can go with a sort of undefined expectation of meeting other interesting people. If there are different demands to be made of a library in the future, then the building is sufficiently flexible to accommodate changing user requirements. But the meeting function, the preserving function, the studying function and the collaboration function will always remain. And for this the library, certainly in its present form, is an ideal spot.

Based on conversations with Aryan Sikkema, director of the building department at the University of Utrecht,and Art Zaaijer, urban design supervisor of De Uithof held a few weeks after the UBU building opened.

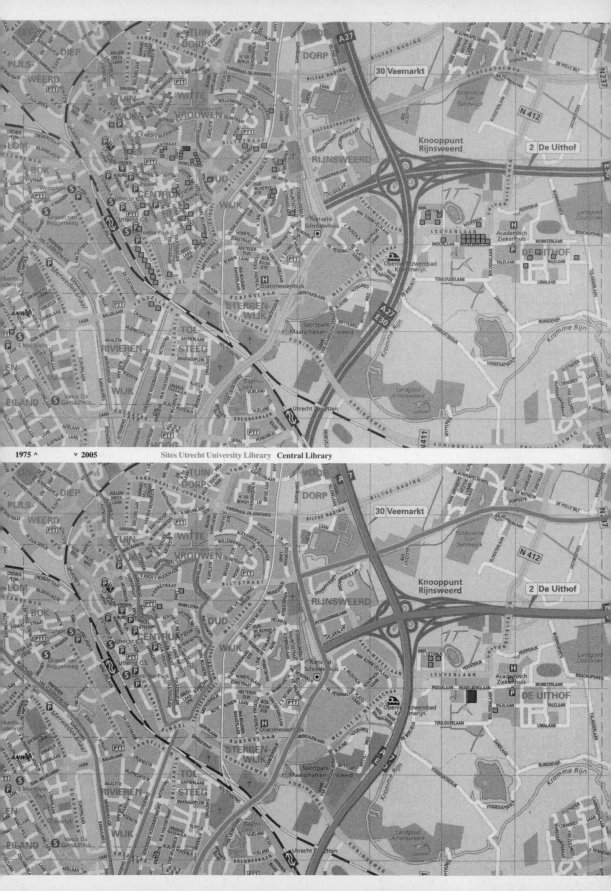

1975 ^   ˅ 2005   Sites Utrecht University Library   **Central Library**

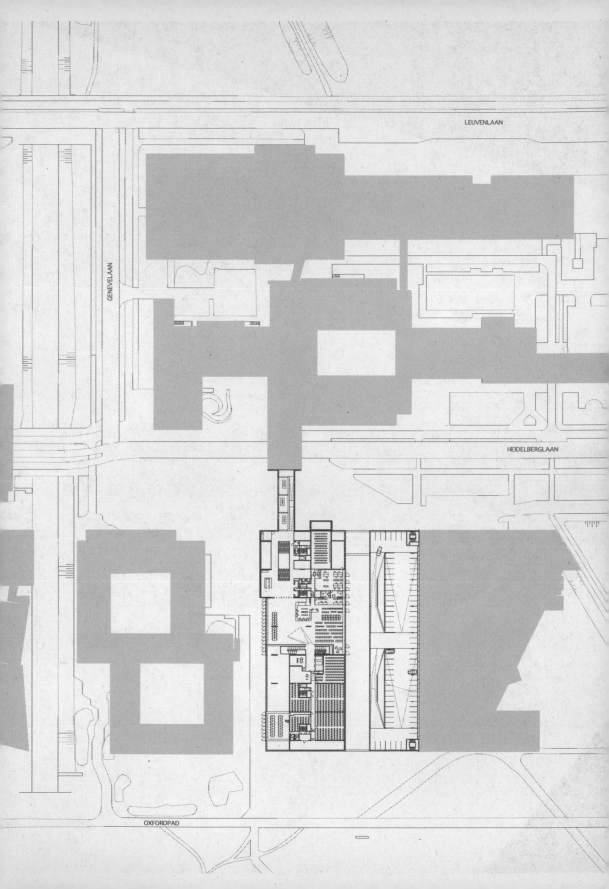

LEUVENLAAN

GENEVELAAN

HEIDELBERGLAAN

OXFORDPAD

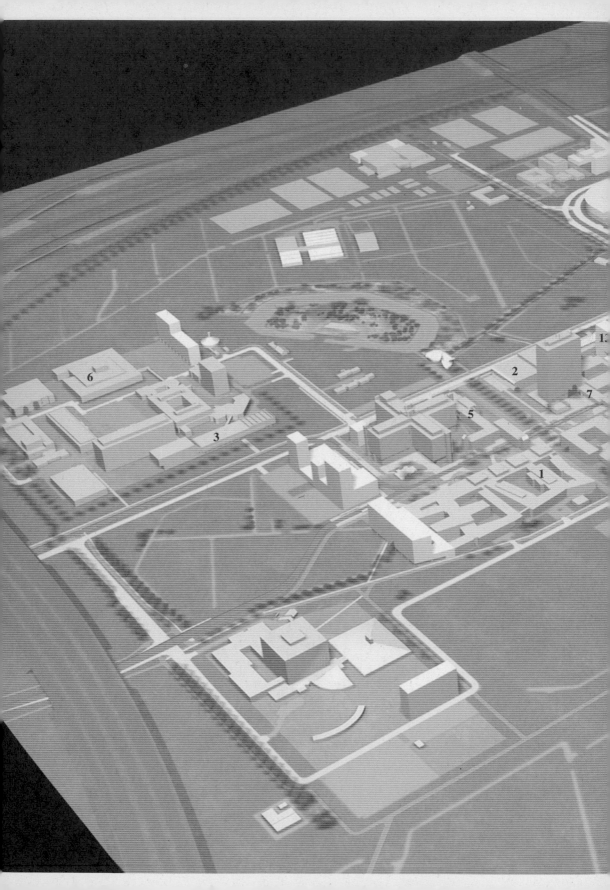

Recent Buildings on De Uithof

1
Faculty of Economics and Management of the Hogeschool van Utrecht (1992-1995)
Architect: Erick van Egeraat, Francine Houben, Chris de Weijer
Mecanoo architecten, Delft

2
Educatorium (1996-1997)
Architect: Rem Koolhaas and Christophe Cornubert
Office for Metropolitan Architecture, Rotterdam

3
Minnaert Building (1997-1998)
Architect: Willem Jan Neutelings
Neutelings Riedijk Architecten, Rotterdam

4
Cambridge Complex (1998-1999)
Architect: Rudy Uytenhaak,
Architectenbureau Uytenhaak, Amsterdam

5
NMR Laboratorium (Nuclear Magnetic Resonance) (1997-2001)
Architect: Ben van Berkel
UN Studio, Amsterdam

6
NITG Building (Netherlands Institute for Applied Geoscience TNO) (2001-2002)
Architect: Jan Hoogstad
Hoogstad Architecten, Rotterdam

7
The Basket Café (2002-2003)
Architect: Walter van Dijk
NL Architects, Amsterdam

8
De Kleine Kikker Day-Care Centre (2001-2003)
Architect: Evelien van Veen
Drost + Van Veen architecten bv, Rotterdam

9
University Library (2001-2004)
Architect: Wiel Arets
ir. Wiel Arets Architect & Associates, Maastricht/Amsterdam

10
ABC Building (Academic Biomedical Cluster) (2004-2005)
Architect: Erick van Egeraat
Erick van Egeraat Associated Architects, Rotterdam/London/
Prague/Budapest

11
Power Station (2004-2005)
Architect: Liesbeth van der Pol
Atelier Zeinstra van der Pol, Amsterdam

12
De Bisschoppen Student Housing Project (2004-)
Architect: Köther & Salman Architecten, Amsterdam

13
Confetti Student Housing Project (2004-)
Architect: Architectenbureau Marlies Rohmer, Amsterdam

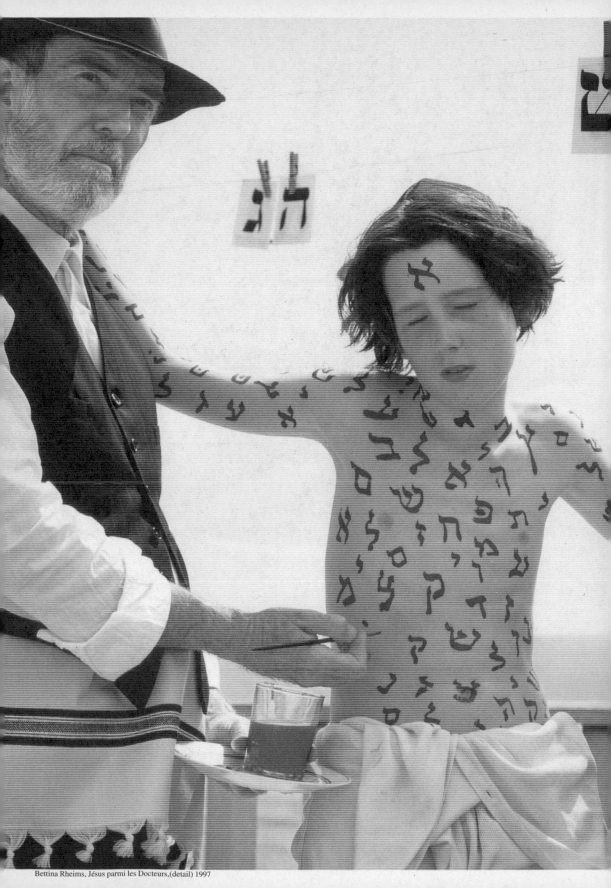

Bettina Rheims, Jésus parmi les Docteurs,(detail) 1997

Peter Greenaway, still from film The Pillow Book, (detail) 1996

WILLOWS ON CONCRETE AND GLASS

**A striking feature of the UBU building is the plant motif on the glass façade
and much of the concrete walls. Inside the building the walls that enclose
the book depots are also covered with a relief of this plant motif.**

The concept of a façade imprinted with a plant motif came about as a result of the 'green zone'
that extends past the library. OMA/Rem Koolhaas had established this zone in the urban plan
and Wiel Arets wanted to go along with this. At the same time the screen print also serves a
technical purpose: the print acts as a sunscreen, but without losing the transparency.

In the design phase we started with four different patterns. It soon became apparent, however,
that this would lead to intrusive cluster-forming of similar panels. We then decided to work
with a single motif and add the same design in 3-D form to the concrete walls. We wanted a
vertical pattern, an image with leaves, not too busy but not too bland either. The photo eventually chosen – of Swedish willow branches and taken by photographer Kim Zwarts – also
has a clear middle point. This gives the façade a certain rhythm. He processed the photo
digitally to enhance the impression of depth.

Concrete panels in relief

Transforming the chosen photo into a 3-D mould for the concrete panels turned out to be
impractical with modern digital techniques. In the end we found the company Adapt-3D, who
saw our problem as a challenge. They specialise in making models for artists. They manually
transferred a print of the image from a sheet of transparent foil measuring about 1.60 by
3.45 metres to a large hard-foamed slab. During this process the various grey tints were
translated into colours and then a fraise depth was assigned to each colour. The darkest tint
was 25 millimetres deep. This was the maximum depth because otherwise too much weight
would be added to the concrete walls. Moreover it would make the rubber moulds too heavy
and unwieldy.

The moulded 'landscape' in the hard-foamed slab was then sanded manually to create a
smooth surface. The result was evaluated by the contractor, by Neoplast, by the firm that
would finally manufacture the rubber moulds, and by us. After some adjustments and
additional sanding, the hard-foamed mould was cast with a hard two-component synthetic
material. This mould was then cast again to create the positive shape. And with this we
finally had a serviceable, hard and strong master mould.

In its factory in Germany Neoplast used this master mould to cast the rubber mats to line the
sides of the formwork for the walls of poured concrete. We first cast some trial mats and carried
out tests with them to find the best way to loosen the mat from the concrete, the most suitable
type of wood to use between the mats, how to insert all sorts of elements such as sockets and
light fittings into the walls, and to develop a general working method. Later on these trial walls
were also used to determine the right shade of black.

Only when we had decided on the right method of work did production of the rubber mats start.
A workplace was set up on site to cut the mats to size. All the walls and glass panels with relief
or print had already been drawn exactly to scale.

The panels in relief inside the building were made on site as the concrete was poured. The
rubber mats with the relief mould were fastened onto a backing formwork structure so that the
mats could be lifted into position by a building crane. An additional advantage of this was that
the expansion of the mats due to heat in the summer was limited. The formwork boards lined
with relief mats were lifted into position and fastened with centre rivets to the opposite side
of the formwork, and then the entire wall was poured in one go. The concrete had to be
vibrated very thoroughly to make sure it filled the entire formwork. The concrete relief panels
on the outer façade had to be prefabricated and then attached to an inner wall that had already
been poured. An insulating cavity behind these panels was also necessary.

Glass panels

The same photo by Kim Zwarts was used for the screen print on the glass façade. Together with Gartner, the firm that built the façade, we looked for a screen-printing firm that could make a screen print of such proportions. First they made trials of a smaller size for both the lighter and the darker parts of the panel. The pattern had to work aesthetically of course from close-by and far away. We aimed for a clear image built up of perfect circles from close-by and a clearly discernible image that suggested depth from a distance. The demands of the actual construction also played an important role here. Because about 50 per cent of the glass surface was printed in white and black, the solar penetration factor of the glass façade had to be reduced from 0.3 to 0.2. The final image was created after various trials with types of screen, manual adjustments, and different shades of white. Once everyone was satisfied with a full-scale mock-up, production could start.

The façade consists of different kinds of reflective and insulating glass. We wanted to give staff and students an unobstructed vista and to frame the view from the reading rooms. That's why moveable shutters with the same plant motif are mounted here and there on the transparent glass façade. Staff can operate them manually, except when there is a strong wind. In the public areas the shutters are centrally controlled in response to the position of the sun and direction of the wind. When open, the shutters project at right-angles to the façade and create a dynamic appearance.

The glazed façade is structurally bonded in its entirety, a technique rarely used in the Netherlands. In the factory the glass panels were bonded to an aluminium profile, which in turn was attached to an aluminium frame. This whole prefabricated assembly was delivered on site and lifted into position by crane. Various tests had been carried out in advance, for example in the climate test chamber. We made a conscious decision not to use the customary clamp frames because they would negatively affect the smooth appearance of alternating concrete and glass panels. The bonded structure was developed in close co-operation with the façade builder, the local authority, certifying and inspection bodies, and the architects. The result is a façade entirely of glass, which does full justice to the plant motif.

Excerpts from a conversation with Harold Aspers, project leader for the UBU,
Wiel Arets Architect & Associates

1400 (gevelstramien)

245   1142   13

R001

P+16650

P+16555   70   P+16580   4   2,7

25

3625

3424

5355

3424   voorzijde relief

3436,7   voorzijde konstruktief beton (voorzijde glaslijn gevel)

3432   achterzijde konstruktief beton

P+13200

P+13130   70   4   2,7

201

R002

1651

370,5   1142   138,5

25   50   50

125

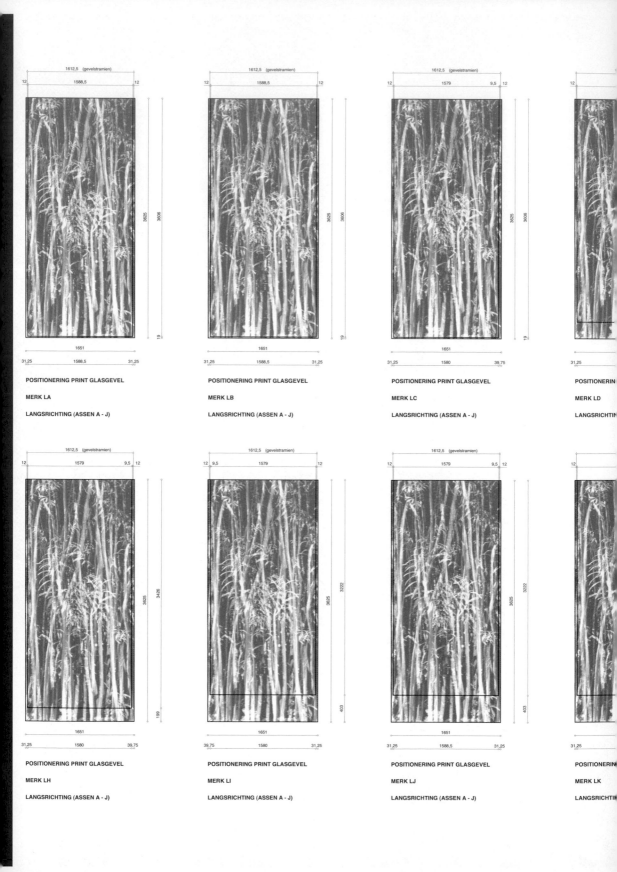

1612,5 (gevelstramien)
12 1588,5 12
3625 3606
1651
31,25 1588,5 31,25

POSITIONERING PRINT GLASGEVEL

MERK LA

LANGSRICHTING (ASSEN A - J)

1612,5 (gevelstramien)
12 1588,5 12
3625 3606
1651
31,25 1588,5 31,25

POSITIONERING PRINT GLASGEVEL

MERK LB

LANGSRICHTING (ASSEN A - J)

1612,5 (gevelstramien)
12 1579 9,5 12
3625 3606
1651
31,25 1580 39,75

POSITIONERING PRINT GLASGEVEL

MERK LC

LANGSRICHTING (ASSEN A - J)

1612,5 (gevelstramien)
12

POSITIONERIN

MERK LD

LANGSRICHTIN

1612,5 (gevelstramien)
12 1579 9,5 12
3625 3426
199
1651
31,25 1580 39,75

POSITIONERING PRINT GLASGEVEL

MERK LH

LANGSRICHTING (ASSEN A - J)

1612,5 (gevelstramien)
12 9,5 1579 12
3625 3222
403
1651
39,75 1580 31,25

POSITIONERING PRINT GLASGEVEL

MERK LI

LANGSRICHTING (ASSEN A - J)

1612,5 (gevelstramien)
12 1579 9,5 12
3625 3222
403
1651
31,25 1588,5 31,25

POSITIONERING PRINT GLASGEVEL

MERK LJ

LANGSRICHTING (ASSEN A - J)

1612,5 (gevelstramien)
12

POSITIONERIN

MERK LK

LANGSRICHTIN

Mulberry Trees growing from Hell
Design Innercourt

De Uithof, as its name suggests, is a green enclosure outside the city, a garden, a campus, by definition contemplative. Within De Uithof, the UBU is certainly such a spot. The patio forms a still life with wistaria, mulberry trees and soft, red seating elements.

The rigorous architecture and the rectangular base of the patio formed an ideal context for an introvert garden. One of the patio walls in front of the parking garage consists of netting that will be covered with a haze of blue wistaria. The rectangular base with large black pebbles will be framed by large concrete tiles with a border of lily-of-the-valley. Under these pebbles 'hell' is visible through red-glowing areas. From this 'hell' grow mulberry trees: vulnerable, gnarled and twisted, and leaning heavily on red crutches. The patio is accessible through the restaurant; in several places there are doughnut-shaped, red seating objects that in summer invite the visitor to become a part of this still life.

West 8, Rotterdam

MORE THAN A GATEWAY
The Role of Future University Libraries

"Well in our country," said Alice, still panting a little, "you'd generally get to
somewhere else – if you ran very fast for a long time, as we've been doing."
"A slow sort of country!" said the Queen. "Now, here, you see, it takes all
the running you can do, to keep in the same place. If you want to get
somewhere else, you must run at least twice as fast as that!"
Lewis Carroll, Through the Looking Glass

Introduction

Libraries are subject to serious change as a consequence of developments in information technology. This is the case both for public libraries and for libraries attached to a parent organisation, such as university libraries. This article presents some thoughts on what the future may hold for university libraries. The role of the library within the university is changing rapidly; information technology is not only pervading the library, but also penetrating the primary processes of the university, research and education. It is a major challenge not only to keep up with these changes, but also to anticipate future developments strategically.

Towards digital libraries

The first wave of library computerisation took place in the 1970s. Manual back-room activities, such as acquisition, distribution and cataloguing, were turned into computer-controlled activities. This period also saw the introduction of various electronic databases, such as local bibliographic and indexing databases. As a result, the library's traditional customers had to reorient themselves on a fundamental level to the new way in which bibliographic information was now becoming available, i.e. through an on-line public access catalogue (OPAC). During the second wave of library computerisation, which started in the 1990s, the focus was on the deployment of computer networks providing access to remote electronic information. Since then, access to electronic information is no longer limited to so-called secondary information (catalogues, bibliographic databases). Primary information has now become available electronically as well. For instance, users have access to the full-text electronic versions of scientific journals. Electronic textbooks and readers enable users to consult information outside the library, i.e. at their professional and private workplaces. All traditional library activities are being affected by this innovation. A number of trends can be identified in this context.

One very important trend is the decreasing prominence of the library's physical collection (mainly printed books and journals), and the corresponding increase in the importance of information reference. The library is a gateway, referring users to information irrespective of the location where that information is physically stored.

A second trend is the integration of library services in the processes that are supported by the library. It is becoming ever more difficult to distinguish between the actual provision of information and the various processes in which that information is used. A university library, for example, is connected to a university, whose primary tasks are education and research. At its most fundamental level, teaching is characterised by the transfer of knowledge from teacher to student. The traditional borderline between knowledge transfer through teaching on the one hand and the provision of information by the library on the other is fading fast owing to the use of information technology in education. To a growing extent, library services are blending with the teaching process. Similar trends can be observed in research processes. It also holds true for primary processes in other types of institutions supported by library tasks, for example in policy-making and legal consultancy.

A third trend is the erosion of the self-evident position of the library in the so-called information chain: the process from information production to information consumption. The role of the library is often described as one link in that chain. In the traditional information chain, the main functions, i.e. the production, distribution, acquisition and consumption of information, were accommodated in strictly separated stages and by different parties. However, the configuration of functions within the information chain has begun to shift. Within this changing constellation, all the parties involved (such as the publisher, the bookseller, the library) are struggling to redefine their positions; many of them are innovating and experimenting creatively with new roles instead of adhering to traditional patterns.

At this time, the full and long-term implications of these developments are far from clear. However, for the first time in history, libraries are confronted with competition. Traditionally, the publisher sold its products to the library, and the library in turn provided services for the 1so-called end-user. Now several publishers are developing services for the end-user as well. Moreover, new products such as – at this moment – Google scholar provide search facilities, seducing people to use the user-friendly simple tools instead of turning to the library. The main competitive advantage the library may have is its direct link to the primary processes of the university and its knowledge of these processes. In that case, this advantage should be treasured and strengthened, because the library's added value for research and education should be real and clearly visible.

Developments in research and teaching

As has been mentioned already, the processes of research and education are changing as a consequence of technological developments. These changes have consequences for the way the library has to perform its role.

In research, the following trends can be observed[1]:
> increasing diversity in the location of research activities;
> increasing focus on interdisciplinary, multidisciplinary and transdisciplinary research;
> increasing focus on problems rather than techniques;
> greater emphasis on collaborative work and on more diverse and informal models of communication;
> greater emphasis on working with primary data in digital form;
> increasing demand for access to a wider range of more diverse sources;
> the need for access to and management of non-traditional, non-text digital objects;
> new needs for information dissemination.

As a consequence of these trends, it is necessary to re-engineer the present system for the creation, production and distribution of scientific knowledge. Easy access to as much information sources as possible is vital. However, researchers also need tools to manage the information they actually use and to support communication with their peers.
The scholarly publishing system is now evolving along two distinct paths[2]. On the one hand, large multinational commercial publishers are increasing their dominance in access to scientific publications. This has led to the so-called serials crisis. Prices of scholarly journals are rising every year by a percentage that is substantially higher than the consumer price index. This leads to the cancellation of subscriptions, which in turn leads to new price rises. Consequently, the traditional system of scholarly communication is becoming unaffordable. On the other hand, there is a worldwide movement towards Open Access publishing. There are an increasing number of Open Access journals, i.e. journals for which the reader does not have to pay. These journals operate using alternative business models: for instance, the author (or his institution) pays for the peer review and/or the publishing of his text. Alternatively, the journal is financially supported by stakeholders that have a serious interest in the continuity of the journal. In addition, many universities are setting up an institutional repository in which the university's publications are collected, preserved and disclosed. There are also dedicated repositories, giving access to publications in a certain discipline. The philosophy behind these repositories is that the content they contain should in principle be freely accessible for everyone.

The teaching and learning processes at a university are also subject to important changes[3].
> A shift is taking place from an emphasis on education to an emphasis on learning. This implies more active forms of learning, such as more problem-oriented learning.
> The dichotomy between distance learning and face-to-face learning is being abandoned. Various forms of blended learning are emerging, which attempt to discover the optimal combination of different forms of learning.
> A change is also taking place in how people see knowledge. What is considered to be important and certain knowledge is much less clear than several decades ago. For education, this means an increased emphasis on essential basic concepts and principles supplemented by teaching students the skills to master the quickly changing knowledge rapidly.
> Finally, the educational objectives are focusing more on developing competencies. University education is increasingly aimed at academic competencies, such as:
>> communicating using new media;
>> searching for, finding and assessing information;
>> using, exchanging, analysing and interpreting data;
>> compiling, organising and synthesising information;
>> drawing conclusions and generalising;
>> being able to work together.

It thus becomes more and more important for students to learn how to access and use scientific information. However, they also have to learn how to integrate different information sources, how to communicate with others about this information, and how to detect existing research communities or build new ones. There is also a growing need for repositories for educational material, such as learning objects: basic electronic building blocks for e-learning, which can be combined and reused in different courses.

The library as a gateway

One of the distinguishing features of the digital library is that it provides access to digital information irrespective of the location where that information is stored. A modern library's policy should aim at making as much relevant information as possible accessible by electronic means.

A library can of course store all relevant information on its own server, but this is generally not particularly efficient unless the data involved is information that has been produced by its own university. Most of the information to which the library provides access is stored on servers run by publishers or intermediary organisations. How can the access to that information be guaranteed? In practice, a number of possibilities can be distinguished.

> Free access. This is the case for many Internet sites, including a growing number of Open Access journals, which are high-quality, peer-reviewed scholarly journals. There are currently 1440 acknowledged Open Access journals. There are also institutional and dedicated repositories as well as free portals which provide an overview of information sources for specific disciplines.
> Full licenses for well-defined user groups. This is the case with most of the traditional publishers. For universities, so-called campus licenses arranged by the library provide access for university staff and students from the workstations at the university, but also from their homes. These licenses tend to be fairly expensive. Some campus licenses are offered in the form of so-called Big Deals: the library pays a fixed amount of money, in return for which access is provided to all of the publisher's titles.
> Licenses for well-defined user groups with a maximum number of concurrent users. An extreme variant of such a license would be to restrict access to one user at one specified workstation. These licenses are seen less and less frequently for scientific information.
> Pay-per-view licenses. The user has to pay for viewing or downloading the article in question. At this moment, this is not a very popular variant with scientific publishers. The costs are still very high (for instance $ 30 per article) and publishers are reluctant to lower this fee in fear of losing turnover.
> No access. This, of course, is the case for information sources with a license fee that is too expensive for an institution. Traditionally, systems of interlibrary loan solved this problem in the print world. Comparable solutions for digital sources are available or will become available in the future.

Ideally, users have access to all sources of information, although availability may be subject to a variety of financial conditions. This ideal situation cannot be achieved unless flexible arrangements are in place between libraries and publishers. Clever combinations between full licenses and pay-per-view may increase flexibility and thus accessibility.

A well-known problem with freely accessible sources is the problem of information overload. This problem can of course be solved by selection. A library presents a selection of these sources that are relevant for the target group to the different communities in its university. This selection should be made with the help of researchers, as they are better equipped to judge the relevance than library staff.

When a library has arranged access, there still remains the problem of information retrieval. Publishers often present their electronic databases with the help of a user interface developed specifically for their own products, and tend to regard that interface as added value. The consequence of this from the user's point of view is that he will have to scan the information sources from different publishers using different interfaces. In other words, if you look for information, you will have to know which publisher is offering it in order to find it. This is highly inefficient from a user's point of view.

This is where the library comes in. The library can play an important role in facilitating user navigation. Traditionally, libraries operate in close contact with their users and communicate with them in order to establish specific user needs. This is important because information retrieval needs may vary between different organisations and also between different disciplines. Chemists would obviously make different types of demands on library services than theologians. The library therefore presents an interface, tailored to its users' needs, which makes it possible to search all information sources in a specific discipline (free-access sources, licensed information and pay-per-view from different publishers) in a single search action.

The result will be that the users during the search process only get answers that are fully relevant to their question, without being swamped by thousands of articles only marginally related to their subject. The system for information retrieval has a digital helpdesk in the background. In cases where this proves insufficient, personal assistance can be offered. When there are new developments and tools in the field of information retrieval, the library will provide instructions and explanations.

The role of the library as a gateway may seem somewhat distant. Nevertheless, in order to excel in this capacity, the library needs to be fully informed of the preferences of the faculty and students. This requires personal contact with the widely diverse target groups. However, to realise the library's potential added value, the library can and must do more.

It is essential in this context that the services mesh seamlessly with the education and research processes, and preferably even be an integrated part of these processes. This may seem to be to the detriment of the library's visible presence, but the alternative is that the client must step outside his own process to consult the library's resources. This is a barrier that will increasingly be seen as a problem. On the other hand, the library will no longer be seen as overhead; it will become a realistic ambition for it to develop into a partner for both faculty and students.

One important task, then, is to support faculty and students in managing their own information and facilitating the communication with their peers and fellow students.

What does it actually mean to support them in managing their own information?

First, the library will ensure that the client has all the relevant sources of information at his disposal. Access alone is not enough to achieve this goal. A personal message will be displayed when something new appears that is relevant to that specific client. The message is defined based on a sophisticated personal profile that the client can adjust as needed. However, the user will want to organise the relevant information and store it in a way that will make it easy to use. In a sense, he wants to create his own bookshelf that will always be available to him. Using portals ("my library"), the library will give each user access to his own selection and structure, but also to additional relevant information, such as news, conferences and job openings. This type of portal can also offer opportunities for interaction, such as discussion forums.

All the tools listed must be developed with the direct involvement of the target group. This use of modern technology will significantly reduce the time that faculty and students need to search for information. That time can be used to assimilate more information, or for increasing direct production.

To supplement this service, the library will offer the following services to facilitate scientific research. The library will maintain an institutional repository: it will collect, disclose and store the scientific output from the university in such a way that everyone has free access to the publications. In this way, the library also supports the open access movement. Where copyrights cause complications (e.g. for monographs), the information can be stored for the time being, while free access can be granted at a later date. The publications are presented on a university website, as well as the site of the relevant research institute and the site of the individual researcher. This is useful for profiling the researcher and his institute and university, but it also increases the impact of the publications. This service can be seen as a new core business for the library and will therefore preferably be financed from the budget that the library receives from the university, which implies offering it to the researchers free of charge. For long-term preservation, the library can enter into a partnership with an organisation specialising in this field. In the Netherlands, that organisation is the Royal Library.

The library may also play a serious role in the management of non-traditional, non-text digital objects, such as primary data and multimedia objects.

Furthermore, the library can offer assistance in scientific communications. Various libraries support scientists by setting up and producing electronic journals, in which the library and the editorial staff work together to assume the traditional role of the publisher. Because such projects use existing infrastructure, it is possible to offer more appealing conditions than commercial publishers. The library will use the Open Access model for such publications as much as possible, so that everyone can have free access. Due to the lack of subscription fees, the necessary funding will have to come from other sources, for instance by means of subsidies, sponsorships, advertising or author payments. Since 2004, the Utrecht University Library has a unit called Igitur for services in the area of electronic publication and archiving.

The library will also offer services to supplement education. Traditionally, libraries play a role in instructions on library use. Much more is needed now; in this context, the librarian should not be the sole instructor, but the teacher's partner. In a partnership with the teachers involved, the library will teach students to work with scientific information, including using that information in their own publications. Student instruction on using scientific information will take place not as a separate training course, but as an integrated component of a relevant part of the curriculum where working with scientific information is relevant. To supplement this instruction, the students need to learn to seek out communities of colleagues who share their interests, but also to create and maintain such communities themselves. This is very important to their future role in scientific communication.

The library will offer the teachers support in compiling digital readers: not only the selection of materials, but also saving, storing and disclosing the information. If desired, a printing on demand facility could be linked to the service. The library will also play a role in storing and disclosing educational material in a broader sense, including e.g. recording guest lectures.

The same applies to the theses that students write for their Master's degrees; the papers can be linked to the institutional repository. Finally, the library will offer advice and assistance in using scientific information in the curriculum. Among other aspects, this concerns the use of parts of the special collections, such as manuscripts and old printed documents. If these materials are used in education, the library can make them available in a digital format. The papers that the students write on these materials can then be enclosed with the digital versions of the documents as added value, to enrich the sources for future users.

Conclusion

Traditionally, a library has a physical collection. It is responsible for the storage and proper maintenance of this collection, as well as its disclosure and availability. For centuries, users could gain access to the documents in the collection by requesting assistance from a librarian. The physical collection is gradually declining in importance. The library's storage function is changing, increasingly concentrating on the scientific output of the university itself. The library ensures that the university community has access to as many sources as possible, even if they are stored elsewhere. The availability of the relevant sources has to mesh seamlessly with the primary activities of the clients. The user will use the tools of the library, in a sense, to create his own bookshelf and organise it in the manner that suits him best. He becomes his own librarian.
   If this will be the future of the library, will we still need library buildings?
Yes, we will need physical libraries for a number of purposes, both now and in the future. One obvious purpose is to house the print collection and other tangible materials, and to create places where people can obtain assistance in their use. Important factors in this context include the specialised collections and associated library services. It should be noted that even if many sources will be available electronically, many documents will be kept for their cultural value, for instance from the viewpoint of the history of art.
The library also provides places where people can gain access to the Internet and the whole range of electronic resources and obtain assistance in their use. There is an ever-increasing need for such access and assistance.
It houses spaces for people to study, to do research; for students, the library building is evolving toward a learning resource centre. It also provides facilities for people to work together, which are increasingly necessary.
Last but not least, library buildings are increasingly evolving to become an agora, a social assembly place where people meet, by appointment or by accident. Both now and in years to come, the building for the future library is certain to be more than a gateway.

Bas Savenije
Director of the Library

Notes
1. Houghton, John, Colin Steele & Margaret Henty (2003). *Changing Research Practices in the Digital Information and Communication Environment*. Department of Education, Science and Training. Australia.
2. Savenije, Bas (2003). Recent developments in commercial scientific publishing: an economic and strategic analysis. DF Revy 26 (8), pp.220-227.
3. Simons, Robert-Jan (2003). ICT in het onderwijs: naar de derde fase? In: surf/wtr, *De vruchten plukken: Trends en visie*. Utrecht 2003.

Jenny Holzer, Various Texts, La Biennale di Venezia 1999, Xenon projection on façade

Gerald van der Kaap, 013, still from the video Automatic VJ Machine, 1998

dags na vieren hun portie spel op het Stationsplein, zoo ver
mogelijk van de school vandaan. Tot vijf uur was het nog
licht, vooral dáar. En eens, het was al kwart voor vijven, kwam
daar Lies Stuurman aangewandeld, groot, langbeenig, wat
aanmatigend, en toch zoo vriendelijk. Op een afstand riep
ze al: „Ik speel wel even met jullie mee.” — alsof er iets goed-
gemaakt moest worden aan deze jongens, die het toch niet
konden helpen, dat de kleine Jan Zijlstra een der hunnen
was. En allemaal voelden ze het zoo, en ieder uitte dit gevoel
op zijn eigen manier: Dirk Touraine door uitgelatenheid, Jan
Breedevoort door een verwonderd en ootmoedig blinken van
zijn bolle oogen. Leendert Meyer door correcte ernst bij het
spel dat nu volgde, en Willem de Weerd, die toevallig mee-
deed, door iets snoevends in zijn houding, alsof hij er eigen-
lijk achter zat, achter deze zuiverende toenadering. En Anton
merkte af en toe wat in zijn keel, — de tranen misschien,
waarop hij bij Lies Stuurman had gehoopt. Toch was hij niet
verliefd op haar, terwijl ze daar op het Stationsplein krijger-
tje speelden, aangevuurd door het buitengewoon lange meisje, dat ze uitdaagden met „Lies! Lies!” — als ze hen pakken
moest; waarop ze dan met haar hoofd dreigde en bedrijvig
wipte van den eenen voet op den anderen. Als ze hém nazat,
was hij gelukkig; wat een trots ook, met zoo'n meisje te mo-
gen spelen dat grooter was en alleen met jongens erbij. Hij
merkte niet, dat ze aan hem den voorkeur gaf bij het na-
zitten, waarom zou ze ook? „Lies!” riep hij, en dan vloog
ze op hem af, maar héel erg hard loopen kon ze toch niet;
het leek meer op een volwassene die met kinderen speelt en
zich dan natuurlijk niet tot het uiterste inspant.
Zoo laat werd het, dat de zon al achter het tramstation ver-
dwenen was; en nog altijd speelden ze daar, met Lies Stuurman, op wie hij niet verliefd zou worden, maar die hij voor
niets in zijn leven had willen ruilen dien middag, tot over
etenstijd, in den avondschemer, toen hun kwetterende stem-
men nog niet tot rust waren gekomen.

III

„Twee'r Freeksplein!”
„Ja, twee'r Freeksplein! Bezjoer!!”

Simon Vestdijk's Personal Library

The library belonging to the well-known and extremely prolific writer Simon Vestdijk
(1898-1971) was loaned to the Utrecht University Library by his widow in 1989. The loan
consists of books and magazines which formed Vestdijk's personal library. His own work
is not included, except for the various magazines and anthologies to which Vestdijk lent his
co-operation. The magazine Groot-Nederland forms an exception in this respect because
his novel Surrogaten voor Murk Tuinstra appeared in five successive issues. Vestdijk used
this prepublication as a printer's proof and made extensive notes on the installments in
the magazine. The novel was published in 1948.

Catalogus van de Bibliotheek Vestdijk, Utrecht, Universiteitsbibliotheek 1995
Groot-Nederland; Maandschrift voor den Nederlandschen stam, January-May 1940

Thomas Mann
◇
Rede
und
Antwort

Thomas Mann
◇

...EL DER WELTFREUN...

KERR

Es sei
wie es wolle,
Es war doch
so schön!

CARL STERNHEIM / DIE KASSETTE

The Resistance Movement at the UBU

Few people know of the unique role that the Utrecht University Library (UBU) played in the Resistance Movement during World War II. Thanks to the efforts of two sisters, espionage material and illegal publications were smuggled out of the country via interlibrary loans. Hanna Kohlbrugge, who went on to become a Professor of Persian and Islamic studies, created a distribution centre for espionage films in the library's bindery and repository. Her sister Hebe, a member of a resistance group in Amsterdam, provided her with the microfilms. As a result of their heroic and remarkably discreet deeds, a substantial amount of secret military information was able to reach the Allies.

Hanna Kohlbrugge was hired by the library in 1938. In addition to cataloguing the Sanskrit collection, she assisted in lending books and processing interlibrary loans. This marginally increased her meagre salary, but more importantly, provided her greater manoeuvrability to carry out clandestine activities. In addition to her sister, two other UBU employees were fellow conspirators: Willem van Ettekoven and Joop Sakkers, the caretaker. The group of four went to work as follows.

Hebe's resistance group was active in helping refugees flee to Geneva along what later became known as the "Swiss Route." Espionage material was also sent along this channel. The group developed microfilms of German airports, landing strips, bunkers and other military posts as well as underground newspapers, and then delivered them to the library. The messenger would request a book about India at the counter, and was subsequently put into contact with Hanna. She passed the microfilms on to Joop Sakkers, who cut them and hid them in the spines of antiquated medical books. If a smuggled book did not get returned, Hanna would renew the lending period.

Ironically, censorship facilitated their efforts. A relatively large number of books (315 of the total of 830 titles censored in all of the Netherlands at the time) were removed from circulation. They were marked with a pink sticker which in some cases has never been removed. Thus if the staff was unable to locate a book, it was often assumed that it had been banned. The absence of smuggled books was therefore less conspicuous. If possible, banned books were sent to Switzerland, as they were unlikely to be missed. Willem van Ettekoven carefully selected titles that he hoped would not raise the Germans' suspicion.

Hanna's boss, the librarian Abraham Hulshoff, who had been unaware of the group's activities, was arrested by the Germans in 1944. They had become suspicious of the book traffic between Utrecht and Geneva, and paid several trips to the library. The Germans were never able to discover who the real perpetrators were, nor how they operated. Hanna was able to go into hiding. Hebe had already been taken prisoner at Ravensbrueck concentration camp at the time of the arrests. She was released in February 1945.

Vreekamp, H., 'Verzet mogelijk dankzij de censuur, de universiteitsbibliotheek in de tweede wereldoorlog' in: Personeelsblad Universiteit Utrecht 1995, nr 7/8, pp. 3-5

UBU Workspace in Depot, ca. 1940

UBU Library Hall, Lodewijk Napoleon's former Ballroom, ca. 1911

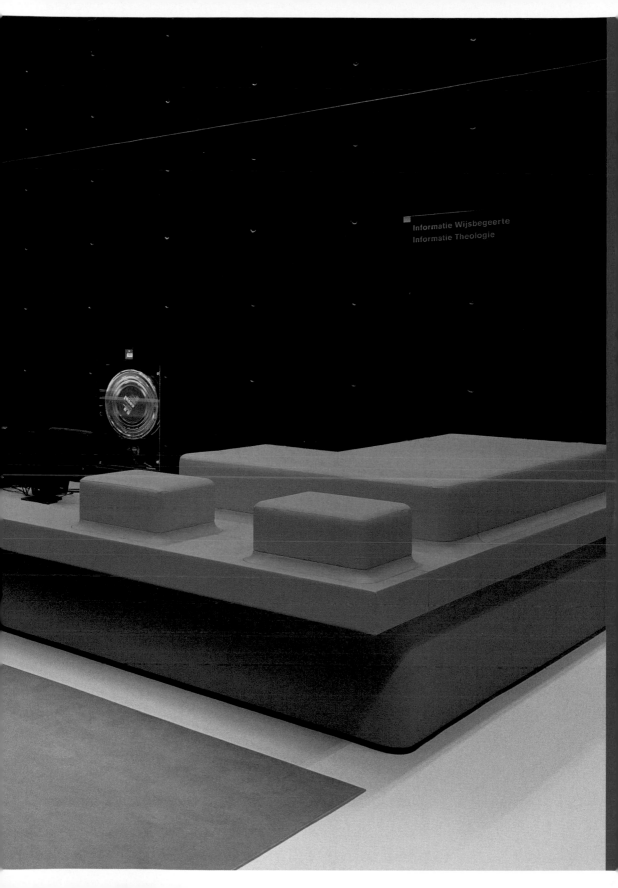

UBU Circulation Desk, ca.1960

UBU Reading Room, ca. 1940

UBU Library in the former chapel of Lodewijk Napoleon, ca. 1940

UBU 'new depots', ca. 1905

ARCHITECT
& Advisors & Contractors

Architect
Wiel Arets Architect & Associates
Project team
Wiel Arets, Harold Aspers, Dominic Papa,
René Thijssen, Frederik Vaes, Henrik Vuust
Collaborators
Pauline Bremmer, Nick Ceulemans, Lars Dreessen,
Jacques van Eyck, Harold Hermans, Guido Neijnens,
Michael Pedersen, Vincent Piroux, Jan Vanweert,
Michiel Vrehen, Richard Welten
Models
Pedro Anão, Nick Ceulemans, Mai Henriksen,
Carsten Hilgendorf, Kees Lemmens, Rob Willemse

Interior design
Custom-made furniture and desks:
designed by Wiel Arets Architect & Associates
produced by Quinze & Milan
Chairs and tables: Vitra
Advisors
Façade print: Kim Zwarts, photographer
Garden architect: West 8
ABT Adviseurs in Bouwtechniek
Huygen Installatieadviseurs
Cauberg-Huygen Raadgevende Ingenieurs
Adviesbureau Peutz & Associates
Wilimas Bouwadviseurs
Adapt 3D
Contractors
Heijmans-IBC Bouw
GTI Utiliteit Midden
Permasteelisa Central Europe

Facts & Figures

Offices: 3,000 m²
Public spaces: 9,000 m²
Depots: 9,000 m²
Technical facilities: 3,500 m²
Commercial space: 300 m²
Parking garage: 12,500 m²
Bicycle storage: 600 m²
Total building area: 38,000 m²
Total building volume: 155,500 m³

Weight of concrete: 33,600,000 kg
Surface of reflective insulating glass with screen-print: 5,500 m²
Height of glass elements: 3.45 m
Surface of concrete with relief:
> cast on site: 2,900 m²
> prefabricated: 2,200 m²
Quantity of black paint: ca. 7,500 litres
Network cabling: 92 km
Max. load of floors in book depots: 1,300 kg/m²

Total size of collection: 76,000 m, including:
> on open shelves: 11,000 m
> in closed depots: 65,000 m

Number of volumes: 3.1 million

65,000 m of books in the depots, including:
> 15,000 m of special collection

11,000 m of freely accessible books and periodicals, including:
> 3,500 m of theology & philosophy collection
> 3,000 m of social sciences
> 2,000 m of general collection
> 1,600 m of geosciences collection
> 1,100 m of manuscripts and old printed books

280 m of not freely accessible maps

In the new library building there is
space for a total of 104.5 km of books

170 staff members
450 parking places
470 work places with network connection
200 workstations
130 seats in the auditorium
3 shops
1 auditorium
1 bar

Building costs: 45,000,000 euro

Utrecht University Library timeline:
> November 1995: start of project
> March 1997: programme approved
> April 1997: selection of architect
> July 2001: start of construction
> May 2004: construction finished
> September 2004: came into use
> March 2005: official opening

Bibliography

Tanja Notten, Bart Lootsma, in *Universiteitsbibliotheek Utrecht. Ontwerp Wiel Arets*, Utrecht 1999.
Janny Rodermond, "Monumenten voor een nieuwe tijd. Recent werk van Wiel Arets", in *de Architect* (2000) 4, pp. 48-59.
Frank Kaltenbach, "Über den Dächern von...- Wiel Arets über sein Konzept der Stadt/On the roofs of...-
Wiel Arets on his Concept for the City", in *Detail* (2000) 5, pp. 806-810.
Hans Ibelings (ed.), *The Artificial Landscape: Contemporary Architecture, Urbanism and Landscape Architecture
in the Netherlands*, Rotterdam 2000, pp. 33-37.
V + K Publishing, "Universiteitsbibliotheek" in *Architectuur Universiteit Utrecht*, Blaricum 2001, pp. 66/67, 79.
Dimitri Waltritsch, "Wiel Arets" in *Il Progetto* (2001) 5, pp. 18-23.
Xavier Costa, "Photographs by Hélène Binet", *Ediciones Poligrafa: Wiel Arets*, Barcelona 2002, pp. 44-53.
Alison Morris, Finlay Paterson, in *Next* Biennale 2002 Catalogue, Venice 2002, pp. 192-95, 336-37, 245 and
in *Next guide*, Venice 2002, pp. 8, 25, 32.
World Architecture (2002) WA 148, pp. 16-109.
Het architectonische Detail, (2002), pp. 30/31.
Hans Ibelings, *The Artificial Landscape*, NAi (2000), pp. 34/35.
Eduardo Souto de Moura, Josep Lluis Mateo, "Revista de Arquitectura e Arte", in *arq./a* (2003) 21, pp. 16, 58-67.
"Nieuwe architectuur" in *Elsevier* (2003) 16, pp. 98-99.
Ludger Fischer, "Bibliothek der Universität Utrecht" in *Baumeister* (2004) 7, pp. 50-57.
Jürgen Tietz, "Alabasterhaut", in *Neue Züricher Zeitung*, Feuilleton 7 Aug 2002.
"De grootste", *Utrechts Nieuwsblad*, 17 Mar 2004.
Bert Heijnen, "Rietstengels als gevelzeefdruk", in *Geveltech* (2004) 5/1, pp. 16-21.
Anka van Voorthuijsen, "Een doos vol boeken", in *Utrechts Nieuwsblad*, 26 Jun 2004, p. 45.
Janny Ruardy, "Een toekomstig museum voor het boek", in *Ublad* (2004) 3 [Sep], pp. 20-25.
Anka van Voorhuijsen, "Een bieb in de wolken", in *Utrechts Nieuwsblad*, 18 Sep 2004.
Wido Smeets, "Wiel Arets: Compromisloos", in *Dagblad De Limburger*, 23 Sep 2004.
Anka van Voortshuijsen, "Je gaat jezelf wel erg klein voelen", in *Utrechts Nieuwsblad*, 11 Sep 2004.
Katharina Mütter, "Der Himmel hängt voller Bücher", in *Süddeutsche Zeitung*, 17 Sep 2004.
"Symposium kunst in de openbare ruimte", in *Gemeente Maastricht*, 2004.
Robert Stiphout, "Superleuke lounge-bieb", in *Elsevier* (2004) 41 [Oct], pp. 24/25.
Prof.Dr.Ir. Gerard Vanzeijl, *Wiel Arets' Bibliotheek: een interventie in de universiteit*, unpublished, 4 Nov 2004.
Katja van der Linden, Rosa Withaar, "Universiteitsbibliotheek leuk, mooi of origineel", in *Punt 05*, 4 Nov 2004.
Massimo Faiferri, "Wiel Arets, Works and Projects", *Electa*, Milano 2004, pp. 186-194.
Harm Tilman, "Ongenaakbaar en tegelijk open", in *de Architect* (2004), pp. 49-57.
Henk Wapperom, "Leermoment in zwart beton", in *Cement* (2004) 8 [Dec], pp. 28-33.
"Constructie laat bibliotheek zweven", in *ABT Nieuws* (2004) 9 [Oct], p. 6.
Josine Crone, "Boekendepots met hangende leeszalen", in *Bouwwereld* (2004) 22 [Nov], p. 52.
Ingmar Heytze, "Universiteitsbibliotheek", in *Illuster, Kwartaalblad voor de afgestudeerden van de Universiteit Utrecht*
(2004) 37 [Dec], p. 24.
Willem Ruyters, "Universiteitsbibliotheek Utrecht: eindelijk voldoende kritische massa", in *Gevelbouw* (2004) 3
[Oct], pp. 14-19.
"University Library in Utrecht", in *Archis* (2004) 6, p. 46.
"Paesi Bassi, Wiel Arets UBU", in *Casabella* (2004) [Dec], pp. 91-105.
Marc Dubois, "Universita di Utrecht: La nuova Bibliotheca di Wiel Arets", in *Casabella* (2004-2005) nr. 728/729.
"Black is beautiful", in *Cement* (2004) 8, pp. 6-9.
Harm Tilman, "Het hele leven moet een feest zijn", in *de Architect Interieur* (2004) [Nov], pp. 32-37.
Olaf Winkler, "Bedrückte Wolken", in *Bauwelt* (2005) [Nov], pp. 32-37.
Billy Nolan, "Rhythm in black", in *Frame* (2005) 42 [Jan/Feb], p. 79.
Roemer van Toorn, "Architectuur in Nederland", in *NAi Uitgevers Catalogus voorjaar* (2005), p. 5.
John Weich, "No more ugly duckling", in *34* (2005) 34 [Dec-Jan], pp. 51-60.
Josine Crone, "Boekendepots met hangende leeszalen", in *Permasteelisa Central Europe B.V.*, (2004) 20
[Nov], pp. 52-61.
"Wiel Arets, University Library Utrecht", in *A+U* (2005) 413 [Feb], pp. 32-41.
"Schwartzbunt, Universitätsbibliotek in Utrecht", in *Deutsche Bauzeitung* (2005) [Feb], pp. 28-40.
"Biblioteca Universitaria Utrecht, Olanda", in *The Plan* (2004-2005) [Dec-Jan], pp. 52-63.
"Utrecht: The gridded exterior of Wiel Arets' library belies the spatial complexity within", in *Architecture Today*
(2005) [Feb], pp. 12-15.
F. Kaltenberg, S. Toonen, H. Cauberg, Y. Uehara, "Universitätsbibliothek in Utrecht, Wiel Arets, Maastricht",
in *Detail* (2005) [Mar], pp. 206-226, 228, 285.
Lukasz Wojciechowski, "Monolit", *Architektur&Biznes* (2005) [Feb], pp. 34-39.
Katerina Jacobcova, "Wiel Arets", in *Beton* (2005) [Jan], pp. 55-57.
Luca Maria Francesco Fabris, "Biblioteca Universitaria a Utrecht (NL)", in *Construire* (2005) [Mar], pp. 38-42.
"Bieb: beangstigend mooi", in *Ublad* (2005) 20 [Mar], UBU Opening special issue.
Robert Uhde, "Das Buch im Schilf", in *Neue Zürcher Zeitung*, 1 Apr 2005, p. 71.
"I live (for) architecture", in *Contractsworld 2005* (2005) [Apr], p. 12.
Aaron Betsky, "Dark clouds of knowledge", in *Architecture* (2005) [Apr], pp. 51-61.
"Universitätsbibliothek Utrecht", in *Best of Europe: color* (2005), pp. 65.
"Schilfgerasel: die schwarze Relieffassade der Universitätsbibliothek Utrecht", in *Opus C* (2005) [Apr], pp. 12-14.
"Wiel Arets", in *Architecture in the Netherlands, NAi Yearbook 2004* (2005), pp. 160-165.
"Architecture in The Netherlands", in *A10* (2005) [May/Jun], p. 21.
"Harmonie tussen verlichting en architectuur", in *Lichtpunt* (2005), p. 3.
Frank Kaltenbach et al., "University Library in Utrecht", *Detail* (2005) nr. 3 [May-Jun], pp. 308-326.
Tracy Metz, "Mobiel bellen op platforms in zwart glas en steen", *NRC Handelsblad*, 10 Jun 2005, p. 6.
Amber van Rijn, "Pronkstuk van De Uithof", in: *CenE Bankiers: Alert* (2005) nr. 2, pp. 48/49.

Photo Credits

Jan Bitter
pp. 3, 4, 5, 6/7, 8, 9, 13, 14, 15, 16, 17, 23, 24/25, 26/27, 34/35, 38, 39, 40, 43, 50, 53, 68/69, 70, 78, 79, 86, 87, 88, 89, 90, 103, 104, 105, 108/109, 110, 113, 114, 115, 116, 117, 124/125, 126/127, 153, 154/155, 156, 157, 158, 173, 177, 178/179, 180, 200, 203, 208, 209, 210, 213, 214, 215, 216, 217, 220, 223, 230, 233, 236, 237, 238/239, 240, 253, 254, 255, 258/259, 260, 262, 263, 264, 265, 266, 267, 268, 281, 282/283, 284, 285, 288, 291, 292/293, 294/295, 296/297,298, 301, 302/303, 304/305, 306/307, 308, 313, 331, 332/333, 336, 341, 342/343, 346, 380, 357, 360, 366, 367, 368, 373, 376, 386, 387, 391, 396/397, 398, 416/417, 418, 421, 422/423, 424, 425, 428, 431, 432/433, 434/435, 436, 450, 454/454, 465

Henryk Gajewski
pp. 28/29, 30, 33, 44/45, 46/47, 48/49, 54/55, 56/57, 58/59, 60, 63, 64-65, 66/67, 73, 80, 83, 84/85, 93, 118-119, 120, 123, 128/129, 130, 174/175, 176, 183, 184, 185, 186/187, 188/189, 190, 224/225, 226/227, 228/229, 234/235, 256/257, 286/287, 309, 312, 314/315, 319, 320/321, 322/323, 324/325, 326, 347, 394/395, 401, 402/403, 404/405, 406/407, 408, 411, 412/413, 414/415, 426/427, 437, 441, 442/443, 446/447, 448

Bas Princen
pp. 36/37 (detail), 159, 160, 163, 164/165, 166/167, 168/169, 170, 388, 438

Wiel Arets Architect & Associates
pp. 133, 139, 140, 143, 144, 145, 146/147, 148/149, 150, 193, 195, 196/197,337, 338, 344/345, 362/363, 364, 365, 369, 370, 371, 372

Pierre Huyghe
p. 199 (based on a photo by Jan Bitter)

UBU Students
pp. 316, 348/349, 392/393

Factordrie
Stills from the video A movement for three dancers, two camera's and a building, choreography Anouk van Dijk, music Lilian Hak, concept and direction Robertjan Brouwer © 2005 Factordrie, Amsterdam
pp. 350/351, 352/353, 354/355, 444/445

Kim Zwarts
p. 356

West 8
pp. 377, 378/379

Ivar Pel, pp. 1, 21, 31, 41, 81, 91, 409

Guto Bussab, Muti Gallery, Johannesburg, South Africa, p. 111

Copulation of clichés, author unknown, coll. Roemer van Toorn, 1997, p. 121

Wim Wenders, still from Wings of Desire, 1987, p. 131

Trinity College Library © The Board of Trinity College Dublin, p. 151

Hiroyasu Sakaguchi, Sendai Mediatheque, Japan, p. 161

Georges Fessy, Bibliothèque Nationale de France, Paris, France, p. 171

Margherita Spiluttini, Eberswalde Technical School, Germany, p. 181

Philippe Ruault, Public Library, Seattle, USA, p. 191 (top); **Wiel Arets**, p. 191 (bottom)

International Libraries © Candida Höfer/ VG Bild-Kunst, Bonn 2005
Candida Höfer:
Librije Walburgskerk Zutphen I, 2003, p. 211
El Escorial VI, 2000, p. 221
Stiftsbibliothek St. Gallen, 2001, p. 222
Playfair Library Hall, University of Edinburgh, 1998, p. 231
Bibliothèque Nationale de France, Paris XIII, 1998, p. 232
New York Public Library IV,1999, p. 241
Stadtbibliothek Stockholm, 1993, p. 242

Michael Kappeler/ddp, Passers-by on the Bebelplatz Bibliothek, p. 279

Recent buildings on De Uithof, map Art Zaaijer Architect, pp. 328/329

Bettina Rheims, Jésus parmi les Docteurs, July 1997, Majorque from "I.N.R.I." published by Albin Michel, Paris, 1998
© Bettina Reims, courtesy Galerie Jérome de Noirmont, Paris, p. 339

Peter Greenaway, still from film The Pillow Book, 1996, p. 340

Jenny Holzer, Various Texts, June 9-13, 1999. Xenon projection on façade. La Biennale di Venezia, Cinni Foundation, Venice, Italy. Courtesy Cheim & Read, New York, p. 389
Photo Attilio Maranzano

Gerald van der Kaap, 013, 1998, still from the video Automatic VJ Machine, p. 390

Hans Mulder, Magazine Groot-Nederland, p. 400

Acknowledgements

The living room of the university
Hans van Leeuwen and the architects of De Uithof

The essay Perspectives with a Piranesian Dimension on page 261 by Marc Dubois was previously published in Casabella (2004-2005) nr. 728/729

Willows on concrete and glass
Harold Aspers, Kim Zwarts

Items about the UBU, its collection and history
Gerard Baltussen, Margriet Blom, Jeroen Bosman, Natalia Grygierczyk, Stephanie Helfferich, Klaas van der Hoek, Nan Klaver, Jan van Kooten Niekerk, Hans Mulder, Pierre Pesch, Elly Reijnders, Daan Thoomes

Maps Utrecht University library sites
Mr. W.P. Heere, Marjo Koelemij, Ron Tichelaar

Vedute
Patrick van der Klooster, Thomas Blits, Mariet Willinge/Hetty Berens (NAi, Rotterdam)

My Future Llibrary
Ties Beek

Paper graphs and info
Jan Enderman

Anna Amalia Library
Jan Simons

Simon Vestdijk's personal Library
Mieke Vestdijk

Wiel Arets Architect & Associates
pp. 19, 94-100, 218/219, 243-250, 271-278, 334/335, 361, 374/375

© Utrecht University Library and
the authors, 2005
© for the reproduced artworks by
the artists and photographers,
their estates, or rights holders
© Wiel Arets Architect & Associates

Prestel Verlag
Königinstrasse 9
80539 Munich
t +49 (89) 38 17 09-0
f +49 (89) 38 17 09-35

www.prestel.de

Prestel Publishing Ltd.
4 Bloomsbury Place
London wc1a 2qa
t +44 (20) 7323-5004
f +44 (20) 7636-8004

Prestel Publishing
900 Broadway, Suite 603
New York, NY 10003
t +1 (212) 995-2720
f +1 (212) 995-2733

www.prestel.com

Library of Congress Control
Number: 2005905470

Die Deutsche Bibliothek holds a record
of this publication in the Deutsche
Nationalbibliografie;
detailed bibliographical data can
be found under: http://dnb.dde.de

Prestel books are available worldwide.
Please contact your nearest bookseller or
one of the above addresses for information
concerning your local distributor.

Utrecht University Library
Heidelberglaan 3
3584 CS Utrecht

info@library.uu.nl
www.library.uu.nl

Editorial Committee
Wiel Arets, Marijke Beek,
Irma Boom, Eva DeCarlo,
Jacques van Eyck,
Bas Savenije

Editor
Marijke Beek

Research
Eva DeCarlo

Texts
Marijke Beek, Eva DeCarlo,
Amsterdam

Design/Image Editing
Irma Boom, Amsterdam

Translations
Jim Tucker: György Konrád essay
Overtaal, Utrecht: Bas Savenije essay
Billy Nolan: Arets/Koolhaas interview
Elizabeth Savage, Paradox Language,
Amsterdam: all other texts

Copy Editing
Billy Nolan, Amsterdam

Printing
Drukkerij Rosbeek, Nuth

Printed in the Netherlands
on acid-free paper

ISBN 3-7913-3455-7